# Abbreviati

CH00690815

| | | | |
|---|---|---|---|
| N | North | ɔ | South |
| E | East | W | West |
| GR | Grid Reference | | |
| FC | Forestry Commission | | |
| NT | National Trust | | |
| OS | Ordnance Survey | | |
| RSPB | Royal Society for the Protection of Birds | | |
| SSSI | Site of Special Scientific Interest | | |
| ⊗ | Suitable for pushchair or similar | | |
| | Suitable for walking stick user | | |

Key to location sketchmaps

━━━━━━ A road or motorway
──────── B road
-------- Footpath
P    Parking

Extent of site (approximate)

River          Canal          Railway

Note:
The publisher and author wish to point out that while every effort has been made to ensure accuracy they cannot be held responsible for location errors or consequences arising from location errors.

# Contents

## Central Warwickshire

## Edge of the Cotswolds

# Foreword

*by*
*Liz Baines, Chair,*
*West Midland Urban Wildlife Trust*

This fascinating and, above all, usable, book cleverly links the wildlife attractions of the countryside to town. This gives you, the people of the largely urbanised West Midlands, as well as you more fortunate country folk in rural Warwickshire, a fine chance to venture into your personally unexplored, or until this book came along unexplained, wild open spaces you might normally consider to be a kind of alien territory with which you have little in common. But in the enlightened company of Peter Shirley, one of our most experienced wildlife watchers and natural historians, you will discover at first hand areas of living countryside on your own doorstep.

With its many humorous touches and intimate word pictures of areas to visit this book will make excellent reading for all keen armchair explorers and wildlife fans, but there is no doubt that Peter's infectious enthusiasm will soon make you get up and about the moment the sky is right and book in hand, start to use it. There is no danger of loosing your way as you are provided with exactly the right quality of tried and tested local detail and down-to-earth descriptions of access to and around the areas involved.

Just be prepared to learn to relax a little in unfamiliar territory and allow yourself to be guided by the keen eyes and confident feet of a real expert—Peter. There really is so much out there waiting for you. Once your first walk is behind you, you will begin to discover a previously unknown world, one that will soon contain a dozen favourite places reserved for favoured visiting family and friends. I urge you to visit these special places throughout the four seasons so you may appreciate their real spirit. Such experiences are a great deal more rewarding and memorable than repeats of even the best TV wildlife programmes!

Eventually you may well wish to know even more about the countryside and its wildlife than this book can provide. Please enquire about the possibility of becoming a volunteer supporter or worker on these very special places at one of the visitor centres available on the larger sites. This very special urban region needs all the help it can get if its sanctuaries (for people as well as wildlife) are to survive into the next millennium and beyond.

# Introduction

## Unmitigated England

This book is about the countryside at the very heart of England. Henry James is reputed to have said:

> *"Warwickshire is the core and centre of the English world; midmost England, unmitigated England."*

The West Midlands (which includes large areas of what was once Warwickshire) and Warwickshire are surprisingly rich in open countryside and superb wildlife sites. These remain largely unknown, except to the locals, for two main reasons. The first is that the industrial conurbation is thought by many to be an unending and dreary succession of factories, roads and houses. This impression is entirely wrong. The second is that there are no dramatic or large scale features, such as extensive forests or uplands.

As far as the West Midlands is concerned, there are many places within the built up area where you can wander at will amongst woods, meadows and lakes, or alongside rivers and streams. These are not just open spaces punctuating the urban fabric, but are genuinely beautiful and - from the nature conservation point of view - important places. Sutton Park is a unique and truly remarkable example of a medieval landscape, the Wren's Nest was Britain's first geological National Nature Reserve, and the meadows of Illey and Lapal have a scale and character lacking from many remote, but intensively farmed, areas of the countryside.

The local authorities, frequently assisted by voluntary agencies and the Countryside Commission, have done all that they can to help people to enjoy these and other areas. There are a number of countryside management schemes, country parks, visitor centres and plenty of leaflets and trails to help you to enjoy your day out.

The lack of prominent geographical features is more of a virtue than a vice. Whilst tourists flock to the internationally renowned centres of Warwick and Stratford, those looking for quieter recreation can easily find it amongst the villages of Warwickshire. The gently flowing lowland rivers, including the Tame, the Sow, the Stour, the Anker, and the Avon, move peacefully through the landscape, disdaining rocky gorges or mountain torrents. No problems here with eroded paths, crowded car parks, or packed "wilderness" areas. This is intimate countryside which rewards patient exploration. Where there are low hills they provide immensely wide views for the minimum effort needed to climb them.

The character of the landscape varies enormously. There are the townscapes of the Black Country, Birmingham and Coventry, the wide flood plain of the River Tame in North Warwickshire, the small fields with their hedgerows and copses in the Arden and North Cotswolds areas and the farms of central Warwickshire with their enclosure hedgerows. Occasional isolated churches, as at Chesterton, are another visible reminder of those enclosures.

I hope that you will be encouraged to explore all this for yourself. To return to the idea of the "Englishness" of the area I will leave you with the words of John Ruskin. Whilst staying in Leamington Spa he wrote these words:

"...the space of surrounding Warwickshire was extremely impressive to me, in its English way... as far as eye could reach, a space of perfect England, not hill and dale—that might be anywhere—but hill and flat, through which the streams linger and the canals wind without lock."

# Using the Book

All of the areas described qualify as "easy" walking places. No steep climbs or scrambles to negotiate and not too much chance of getting lost. Even so some agility is required in places, especially where stock proof boundaries have taken precedence over access for walkers. Easy walking or not, wet grass and mud can be abundant in good farming country so suitable footwear is essential. The vagaries of the English weather also mean that it is best to err on the side of caution with water and windproof clothing. Bear in mind that a dry path in the summer can be a quagmire in the winter, and conversely a wide path along a field edge in the winter can be a tangle of brambles and nettles in the summer.

The areas provide opportunities for every sort of walking, from a gentle stroll to a day long hike. They also vary from tiny gems of countryside, almost hidden within the industrial conurbation, to open hilltops with panoramic views.

Within the two counties covered by this book there are no great geographical features which would naturally serve to divide these walks into different areas. The Birmingham Plateau, the plain of central Warwickshire and the northern edge of the Cotswolds are subtle rather than obvious elements of the landscape, and there are no great forests or dramatic river valleys. For this reason I have split the walks into five groups according to their locations. These five groups are:

**The Black Country:**
A cluster of generally smaller areas in Dudley, Walsall and Sandwell, with one interloper from Birmingham (the Woodgate Valley) tucked into the south-western corner.

**Birmingham and North Warwickshire:**
A variety of places including country parks, the restored gravel workings at Kingsbury and the incomparable Sutton Park.

**Arden and Coventry:**
Places on the fringe of the West Midlands other great city, and in the fascinating area between Birmingham, Coventry and Stratford.

**Central Warwickshire:**
The villages and fields, rivers and woods of the fertile farming country in the heart of the county.

**Edge of the Cotswolds:**
The most rural and most beautiful part of Warwickshire with gently rolling countryside, fine churches and handsome villages.

## Finding the Sites

A sketchmap of the two counties is printed at the back of the book. This gives the locations of all of the areas described and main routes.

Location sketchmaps - sometimes with more than one site indicated - appear throughout the book. These show the position of the sites in relation to main roads and, where appropriate, railway stations. The scale of these varies according to the area of the sites included. Some are "pocket handkerchief" sites, others cover extensive areas of countryside. The dotted boundaries are indications of the area of interest and not necessarily of public access. In many parts of Warwickshire access is limited to public footpaths. It is a sad reflection of modern life that there are more areas of open countryside legally accessible to the public in the Black Country conurbation than in rural Warwickshire.

It is assumed that most people will be using cars to reach the walks, especially in the remoter areas of countryside. For this reason the main map reference given at the start of each walk indicates a parking place. These are not always formally designated. It is sometimes only possible to park in village streets or lanes. Where this is the case please do so considerately, and remember that narrow lanes often have to cater for wide farm machinery. Bear in mind too that field gates are not unofficial laybys but entrances and exits which may be in use at any time of the year.

All of the research for this book has been done using Ordnance Survey 1:50000 Landranger maps, although the Black Country sites will be more easily located using an A to Z. (No references from these are given because there are a number of different editions. The most useful is is the hard bound colour "Master Atlas of Birmingham and the West Midlands" published by Geographers.) Three of the Ordnance Survey maps are needed: No. 139 Birmingham and Surrounding Area; No. 140 Leicester and Coventry Area; No. 151 Stratford-Upon-Avon and Surrounding Area. The northern part of Chasewater is on map No. 128 Derby and Burton Upon Trent Area.

Where they are available you may prefer to use the 1:25000 Pathfinder series of maps, but they are by no means necessary. The majority of sites are either waymarked, have public footpath or bridleway signs or have open access. Where public footpath signs are non-existent (or, as in some cases, lying in hedge bottoms) the generally open nature of the countryside and the accuracy of the Ordnance Survey maps should prevent you from getting lost.

**The Descriptions:**
Each area is described in the following way.
1. Name: e.g. "Napton on the Hill and The Grand Union and Oxford Canals". This line may also have walking stick and wheel symbols, indicating that the area is suitable for the less able and for those using push chairs.

2. Map reference: the Landranger map number followed by the six figure reference (accurate to one hundred metres) with the easting and northing separated by an oblique slash. For example Napton's reference is: MAP 151 REF. 464/612.

3. Location and parking information, including road numbers and nearest large town or village.

4. A summary of the type of countryside and walking involved.

5. The main description, including directions where appropriate. These descriptions are meant to convey the spirit of the places, to be impressions rather than catalogues. They are of necessity brief. People interested in wildlife, architecture, history, or any other aspects of the countryside, will notice, or know where to find out, far more than I could hope to convey in these passages.

6. Where a site is designated (i.e. as a Site of Special Scientific Interest or a Local Nature reserve) this is indicated.

Whether designated or not please treat all areas with respect. Remember that most of the countryside, especially in Warwickshire, is important farming country. People's livelihoods depend upon good management of the land. Open gates, poor parking, disturbance of livestock, trampling of crops and noisy passages through farmyards are all things that farmers can not only do without, but which harm their living.


**Other Information:**
There are brief references to three waymarked long distance footpaths. In addition there are lists of places to visit, organisations associated with the countryside, and other books which will add to the enjoyment of your explorations.

# Chasewater

MAP 139 REF. 036/071

Entrance signposted off the A5 about 1.5 miles north west of Brownhills, close to trotting track. Open until dusk each day.

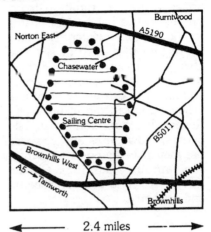

*The largest body of open water in the West Midlands, Chasewater is the "header" pool for the canals of the Black Country, especially the Wyrley and Essington. It is famous for wintering waterfowl and gulls. The pool is bordered by important wetland and heathland where orchids and sundews may be found. The paths are mainly flat although they are narrow and often waterlogged in places. Car park and toilets on the south shore close to the main entrance*

Chasewater is encased by the trappings of modern life. Roads, houses and factories crowd in upon it, and speedboats and sailing dinghies ruffle its waters. Despite this, genuine feelings of wonder and awe, of experiencing a wilderness or a timeless spectacle can be yours if you choose the right moments to be here. Those moments will usually be during a winter dusk, when a lowering sun shoots scarlet darts through winter clouds, and thousands of gulls

rise as one to wheel mewing over the darkling water. If you are lucky enough to witness this from the north shore then you may feel that you are in a truly wild place.

Yet Chasewater did not exist until 1844. It was built for no more romantic a reason than to supply water to the canals which carried the coal, limestone, and iron of local industry. It was created amidst the heathland skirting the ancient Cannock Forest. Winter may be the most spectacular time to visit but there is plenty of interest all the year round. Even so summer weekends are best avoided if it is quiet recreation that you seek.

Fragments of that heathland still remain, particularly on the opposite side of the pool to the car park. A causeway to the north

7

(past the speedboat club) leads between Chasewater itself and a smaller pool (called Jeffery's Swag) to this far shore. Here there is an excellent example of an ecotone - a gradation from one distinctive habitat (dry heath) to another (open water). Between these two it is easy to see the changes through damp and then marshy ground, to willow scrub, and finally to carr where all of the willows grow in the water itself. Rushes, heather, cranberries, bilberries, crowberries and cowberries may all be found here, as may the famous "Cannock Chase berry" - a hybrid between bilberry and cowberry.

This was known to Charles Darwin whose family came from nearby Lichfield. The great man himself may have botanised here as the area - then known as Norton Bog - has long been famous for the variety of plants to be found. Who knows but that Lichfield's other famous sons, Doctor Johnson, David Garrick or Elias Ashmole (for whom the Ashmolean Museum in Oxford is named) did not spend some of their summer afternoons dodging the adders which no doubt lived here then. It is said that Charles Darwin's father Erasmus used to dodge the company of Doctor Johnson because he could not get a word in edgeways with him!

*The insectivorous sundew*

8

Some parts of the area surrounding Chasewater are acid bog. They are ideal places for one of this country's most curious plants - the sundew. This is very fussy about where it grows, only thriving in the poor conditions of acid bogs and moors. Sundews make up for the lack of nutrients in the soil of places like this by turning the tables on its insect visitors. Whereas most plants suffer from being eaten by insects, the insects which alight on sundew leaves suffer from being eaten themselves as the leaves enfold them. And those leaves are very attractive to them, covered as they are with sticky hairs exuding sweet liquid. A mean trick but one which enables the plant to succeed where very few other plants can do so.

If you are visiting Chasewater in the summer then you may be rewarded with gentle flights of butterflies. Common blues and small heaths abound, together with their larger cousins the meadow browns, small tortoiseshells and red admirals. Less gentle are the flights of dragonflies, but the small pools and waterways of the area attract many of them too.

Always though, it is the birds of Chasewater which again and again take your eyes back to the shoreline and to the water. Depending on the time of the year and the time of day you could see any one of more than 200 different species. Busy little waders like dunlin and sanderling at the water's edge, statuesque lapwings, elegant common sandpipers or greenshank, or even an occasional godwit, may accompany your walk. In 1988 the first little scaup (a type of duck) ever to appear in Europe chose Chasewater for its debut. One of the specialities here is goldeneye. These handsome ducks gather every winter. They have characteristic triangular-shaped heads, and the drakes have a prominent white spot beneath their "goldeneye". They are attracted by the deep water (they can dive to depths of 20 feet or more) and the abundance of crustaceans, their favourite food. (Chasewater is home to a large population of freshwater crayfish).

The gull roost can contain as many as 15,000 birds. They are mainly common species, but scores of spectacular great blackbacked gulls may be present together with rarities such as glaucus or Icelandic gulls. In hard weather the warmth of the birds' bodies helps to keep the centre of the pool from freezing over. This means that species like the goldeneye can continue to feed.

Chasewater is one of those special places where human activity has if anything enhanced the conditions for wildlife. It certainly provides a sort of natural theatre where there is a free show every day, the cast is never quite the same two days running, and the scenery can be superb.

# Cotwall End Valley and Turner's Hill

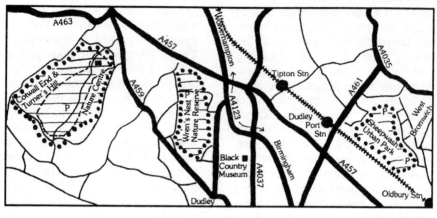

◄──────────────── 6 miles ────────────────►

**MAP 139 REF. 910/923**

Car park in Cotwall End Road Sedgley about one third of a mile south of Cotwall End Nature Centre, or at the Nature Centre itself where refreshments and toilets are available. There is a small charge for parking at the Centre, but not at the other car park. Cotwall End Road is off the A463 from Sedgley to Wombourne.

*This gentle stroll takes in a variety of landscapes on the western fringe of the West Midlands. Old fields and woodland with steep-sided stream cuttings contrast with open views across Shropshire and the Black Country. Although the paths are generally good there are difficult places where mud has been puddled in field gateways, or where long flights of steps have been built. A network of paths leads away from the car park in every direction, so you can wander as fancy takes you.*

In winter the car park welcomes you with hazel catkins dangling over a little stream just where another stream skips down the hillside to join the first. Wrens and robins sing from the thickets and crows and magpies occupy the tree tops. If you venture into the wood (going north-east towards the Nature Centre) little steep-sided valleys await you, each with its own rippling, riffling, running rill. A number of large bowl like depressions will also be found, the origins of which I know not. They

10

seem to be too big to be the remains of charcoal burners' pits, and to be the wrong shape for old coal diggings. On the other hand they do not appear to be natural features. As you move up the hill the wood gives way to open pastures grazed by horses. Some of these fields have never been agriculturally improved. In the summer they play host to many wild flowers - such as meadow buttercup, yellow rattle, tormentil and heath bedstraw - which have been squeezed out of that mythical place "the countryside" - but which retain a toehold here on the edge of town.

Looking across the pastures an unattractive concrete fence marks the boundary of Cotwall End Nature Centre. Best to either go inside the Centre to enjoy its attractions or, perhaps, to look west when a clear day will reveal some of Houseman's "blue remembered hills" of Shropshire. The Centre is run by Dudley Council. It covers about 15 acres (6 hectares) and has many attractions, including a variety of small animals and birds, a craft centre and a play area.

By the southern entrance to the Centre an ancient and massive horse chestnut pollard leans confidentially over a stream, pointing the way towards the farmyard opposite. A public footpath leads through this and across the golf course which now occupies the farm fields. The hedge alongside the path is more than just the standard hawthorn hedge so often encountered, and includes a fair amount of regenerating elm.

The course looks as if it has just been dropped on to these fields and this gives it a welcome natural appearance. It is to be hoped that the members do not allow themselves to be influenced by American golf courses as seen on television. If they do a manicured, artificial landscape will be imposed upon the hillside, and the present character will be destroyed. A disadvantage of taking the footpath (apart from flying golf balls) is that it leads on to the Straits housing development. Whilst this allows a close view of some attractive gardens adjacent to the path, it makes for a tedious ten minutes walk to regain the woodland opposite. It is a pity that the path could not have been diverted across the school playing fields to avoid this.

The southern end of Turner's Hill provides an open area of scrub and grassland with a few outcrops of sandstone. (The geology of this small area is quite complicated. It includes the western boundary fault of the South Staffordshire coalfield). Blue tits and bullfinches may be seen foraging amongst the branches of the trees and bushes, and wild roses guard the path edges. A nice touch is provided by local horse riders who have created a small jump between two big trees - appropriately enough they are horse chestnuts. The woodland on the hill displays its ancient origins with springtime flowers which include bluebells, wood anenome, yellow archangel and wood speedwell.

11

# Wren's Nest National Nature Reserve

MAP 139 REF. 937/922

A wooded limestone hill one mile north of Dudley town centre. The site is surrounded by housing in the area between the A459 (Priory Rd.) and the A4168 (The Broadway). Wren's Nest is the West Midlands County's only national nature reserve (Warwickshire is without). Car parking by the Caves Inn in Wren's Hill Road close to Mons Hill School.

*A small but fascinating site in the heart of the Black Country. It offers an internationally important geological area, an abundance of wildlife and extensive views over the surrounding area. Good paths, but unsuitable for wheelchairs as there are a number of long flights of steps. Two things to remember here: first, do not take fossil hammers into the reserve, or remove fossils; second, limestone quarrying has left parts of the hill in a dangerous state, do not venture into the old quarries or caves.*

A pair of goldfinches work their way through hawthorn and young sycamore festooned with the red and orange berries of black bry-ony. From deep in the tangled undergrowth a little wren pours out its big song. The muted hum of traffic drifts up the hillside from the busy streets below, seeming to be both close by and distant - almost as if intruding from another world. That just about sums up the Wren's Nest. It is an oddity, an impossible place. Closely packed houses fringe its lower slopes, forcing it to occupy the only place left, the space between the ground and the sky.

The entrance to the reserve is somewhat unprepossessing. A grand sign announcing that it guards the main entrance sits disconsolately between the inn and the school. It looks as if it would be more at home deep in a forest, or by the side of a mountain pass. You should not be put off by this unpromising start. A network of good paths will take you around both Wren's Nest Hill and Mons Hill on the other side of the road. Self-guided trail leaflets are available from Dudley Council's libraries and museums. The best way to enter the reserve is in fact to ignore the "main entrance" sign, go past the inn and take the path below the cliff face. This brings you to a spectacular outcrop of limestone which has obviously been forced up from its original position.

The fame of Wren's Nest results

12

from the abundance of fossils found in the limestone - Dudley town's coat of arms includes an heraldic trilobite christened by locals "the Dudley Bug". This reserve was the very first national nature reserve designated (in 1956) for its geological interest. Although now lying at one of the high points of the Black Country the rocks you see around you were once at the bottom of a warm ocean. In places the limestone is clearly layered, reflecting the conditions when they were formed about 400 million years ago.

The main trail winds around the edge of the hill (another incongruous feature - or would geologists call it a discontinuity? - is that the flat centre of the hill is laid out for football pitches) past the entrances to old limestone mines. The safety fence is an ugly, but presumably necessary, intrusion into an otherwise very attractive area. It keeps people away from the steep shafts disappearing into the stygian darkness. Far below lies not the Styx, but a canal. How better to get the limestone away in the 19th. century than by

putting a canal under the mine? There are now five pillars of limestone holding up the top of the hill. At one time there were seven, known as the seven sisters. The fact that two of them have collapsed is a reminder of the instability of these old workings.

Where the path goes around the southern end of the playing fields there is a good view of Dudley town, with the castle ruins looming over Castle Hill. This too is a limestone outcrop, but Rowley Hills, with their radio masts peeping from behind the castle, are made from an entirely different mineral known as "Rowley Rag". The old limestone workings on Castle Hill now house exotic animals from all over the world in Dudley Zoo. To the left of the castle the flat plain of the Black Country stretches to the east, littered with the paraphernalia of industry and commerce.

When you have admired the views and pondered on the 400 million year history of the Wren's Nest you may focus more closely on the here and now. Almost as a bonus the two hills (Wren's Nest

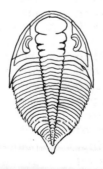

*Trilobite fossil*

and Mons) offer natural history delights as well. Being limestone ash does well here, but beech, oak and sycamore are also found. Many of the trees were planted by the Earl of Dudley in about 1815. This was an early effort at "greening and screening", an attempt to soften the impact of limestone quarrying. Signs of much older woodlands remain as well. Bluebells, dog's mercury and wood anenome carpet the ground in spring. Birds flit through the trees all the year round, and in winter the bryony berries compete with the hawthorn berries, the rose hips and the brilliant scarlet berries of guelder rose for the attentions of both the walker and the thrush.

A remarkable tourist attraction close by is the Black Country Museum. Whole buildings have been taken down and re-erected at the Museum to recreate a complete Victorian industrial village. The history and culture of the Black Country is there to be experienced as first hand.

# Sheepwash Urban Park    | ⊕

MAP 139 REF. 976/921

Car parking just off Sheepwash Lane which runs between the B4166 and the A461 just to the south of Great Bridge, in Tipton. No facilities on site yet, but car parks and toilets are planned. Alternative parking may be found in Anne Close, off Dunkirk Avenue (Map 139 REF. 978/916).

*This is an area of reclaimed industrial land covering about 80 acres. The landscape is still very young, much of the work having been carried out in the 1980's. It would be false to claim that you will enjoy a countryside experience here, but there is much of interest. The new planting, the excellent bird life and*

*the links with the Black Country's history, combine to provide both a glance at the past and a glimpse of the future. The site is typical of so many in built up areas where the use of the land changes from century to century. The paths are wide and easy, the slopes are gentle.*

If this is not countryside neither is it orthodox parkland as the name may suggest. Sandwell Council are working hard to create a naturalistic landscape. They have planted thousands of trees, sown millions of flower and grass seeds, and reprofiled the pools and banks. It is now possible to escape very quickly from the surrounding houses and factories and enjoy a quiet afternoon contemplating the birds on and around the pools. Over 100 species now

14

visit Sheepwash every year. The list includes flycatchers, curlew, little ringed plover and common sandpiper. One of the more innovative pieces of habitat creation is the building of a sandstone cliff face in the hope of attracting breeding sand martins.

Being close to Tipton - which is known as "the Venice of the Midlands" on account of its miles of canals, rather than because of its stunning architecture or art treasures - you would expect a canal to be somewhere close by. In this case the canal is above your head, not where you usually expect to find a water course! It shares the high embankment which forms the south-western boundary of the park with the main railway line between Birmingham and Wolverhampton. Hopefully there will never be a repeat of the incident which occurred here on the 9th September 1899 (9/9/99) when a hundred yards of canal towpath gave way and millions of gallons of water swept into the marlpit. That marlpit was the basis for the large pool you see now. It may be that in the deep mud below the surface some of the canal boats which were swept from the canal still lie. The local newspaper reported on stranded and up-turned boats, narrow escapes & the flooding of two acres of meadow.

The name Sheepwash suggests that at some time this area was grazed by sheep, and that perhaps the River Tame, which flows across the site, supplied water for a sheep dip. This is the Oldbury arm of the Tame, and it has been treated very unsympathetically by the engineers. It has been picked up and moved more than once. Today its engineered channel is not even softened by vegetation as the banks are kept close mown. What a difference from the scene that would have greeted you here a few centuries ago. Then a water mill stood on the river, every turn of its wheel providing a bit more income for the monks of Sandwell Priory. When that house was founded part of its income came from the mill at "grete" - now Great Bridge.

Rural pursuits held sway until the 18th. century (indeed the Ordnance Survey map of 1887 shows that then there was still a John's Lane Farm in the western part of the site, presumably the flooded meadows referred to above belonged to this farm). Even so the demands of local industry caused great upheavals. Coal mining, sand and clay extraction, brickworks, the building of the railway and canal, all played their part in changing the landscape. For about 250 years industry had its wicked way with Sheepwash leaving scars and contamination. Now the wheel has nearly turned full circle and once again the meadow pipits rise tseeping from the grass, swans raise their cygnets on John's Lane Pool, and you and I can enjoy a walk amongst the trees and flowers of the Tame Valley.

# Fens Pools & Buckpool Wedge

## MAP 139 REF. 899/870

Car park (signposted for "nature trail") at Buckpool School, Brierley Hill Rd. one-and-a half miles north of Stourbridge town centre. Brierley Hill Rd. is the B4180 which runs between the A491 and the A461. Alternatively there is a car park at Fens Pool Community Centre, Chapel St. Pensnett (map ref: 917/888).

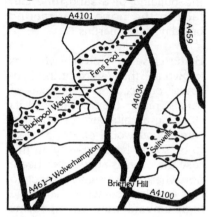

◄──────── 3.6 miles ────────►

*A long finger of land to the west of Dudley rich in wildlife. Nearly all reclaimed from colliery heaps, refuse tips and disused canals this area has been described as "astonishingly rich" in wildlife. The land in the north east, which includes the main pools, is an SSSI because of its value to amphibians. The species breeding there include frogs, toads, smooth newts and great-crested newts. Dudley Council manage the whole area. Good paths have been laid out (although there are one or two places where steps have been built or where there is a lot of mud) and leaflets are available.*

There are many places on this walk which it would require very rose-tinted spectacles to describe as "pretty". There is however a great deal of wildlife, some charming corners and sweeping views over the neighbouring Staffordshire and Worcestershire countryside. Surveys by the Urban Wildlife Trust in the mid-80's revealed over 200 species of wildflowers and nearly 90 different sorts of birds in this mosaic of habitats. These habitats have resulted from a variety of apparently unpromising previous land uses. The canal builders and coal masters of the 19th. Century, and the waste disposal officers of the 20th. bequeathed a legacy richer than they could have imagined. What were their reservoirs, slag heaps and tips are now home to such rarities as adder's tongue fern, southern marsh orchid, true bulrush, wood club-rush, great-crested newt, redpoll, greenshank

16

and jack snipe.

Staff and pupils at the Buckpool School have worked hard to look after their end of this wonderful green wedge. The school nature area lies between the car park and Buckpool Gully. From the car park walk around the left hand side of the school buildings through the young plantings, with bracken covered slopes rising to the left and in front of you. The path down into the gully is reached either through a chain-link gate in the school fence or through a kissing-gate by the road.

Here a stream lies beneath steep banks covered in ash, hazel and hawthorn. One hazel in particular, unusually large for this species, reaches out from the far bank to hang its catkins over the water. In another place a fallen oak dips its gaunt fingers into the cool waters. The stream falls musically over little weirs which control its fall on the way to the River Stour. The weirs may be man-made, but if you close your eyes the sound of tumbling water can transport you to distant mountains and moors where a hundred such becks and rills cascading across rocks and stones sing the same song. A bird often seen in those uplands - the grey wagtail - may be seen here, or along the nearby Stourbridge Canal. The enclosed gully isolates the walker from nearby housing and industry, and brings the birdsong, the butterflies, the dragonflies and the flowers that much closer.

The path takes you up on to the Leys where you will find a flat open landscape with blocks of newly planted trees. One or two horses are likely to be grazing here with heads down, studiously ignoring the view out to Kinver Edge. Turn right at the canal and then left over the bridge to walk with the disused canal on your right. Here natural succession from open water to marsh is well advanced. False bulrush dominates the old channel with its cigar-like seed heads. More unusually greater knapweed grows in profusion close to the path.

Behind the Dell playing fields tall willows line the opposite bank, making do with the canal whilst pining for a river. Over the road and you and the trees change banks. Now the natural looking willows have been replaced with members of the monstrous regiment of Lombardy poplar which marches in small platoons across the urban landscape. This part of the old canal is called wide waters. In late winter kick-boxing coot squawk defiance at each other as they sort out their domestic arrangements for the summer.

Still rising the path arrives at the three large pools - Grove, Middle and Fens. Unfortunately there is no proper path to take you around Fens Pool, although in the winter it is possible to scramble around the scrub-covered far bank. On a clear day the distant Malvern Hills can be seen to the south west, with the Clee Hills and the Wrekin to the west and

17

north west.

The pools are old canal reservoirs and teem with birds all the year round. The wintering waterfowl look especially attractive on a crisp sunny day in December or January. Tufted duck, mallard, pochard, goldeneye and mute swans mingle with great crested grebe, moorhens and black headed gulls. In the spring and autumn migrating birds of every sort make Fens Pools a bed and breakfast stop on their long journeys. Waders and terns, songbirds and raptors, all take advantage of the facilities on offer.

It is possible to vary the route back by walking along the Stour-bridge Canal towpath instead of across the Leys. This brings you close to a number of factories but also allows you to see the neat re-furbished locks on the navigable part of the canal. Their blue brick surrounds and black and white lock gate tops have been restored to their former glory. There is also a good chance of seeing grey wagtails in this area. Whether you see these birds or not the sight of the Samson and Lion pub indi-cates that you are nearly back at the car park.

# Doulton's Claypit and Saltwells | ⊕

MAP 139 REF. 934/870

Two miles south of Dudley. Turn left at Merry Hill round-about on the A4036, then left again at the sign for the Saltwells Inn, car park at end of drive. Car park free, open until late afternoon. Field centre on opposite side of the wood.

*A unique mixture of natural history, local history, modern recreation management, and geology, contained in a varied site in the very heart of the Black Country. Plenty of easy walking through centuries old woodland, abandoned (but naturally recolonised) mineral workings, and around a canal reservoir. In*

*1981 declared the first Local Nature Reserve in the West Midlands County by Dudley Council.*

This is a most remarkable place. Scarred by the Industrial Revolution, exploited for the coal, clay, and salt found beneath the ground, yet still attractive, and still drawing the people of Dudley to itself as it has done for hundreds of years. They come now to enjoy the dark seclusion deep in the wood, to admire the orchids in the bottom of the claypit, or to watch the boats on Lodge Farm Reservoir. In the last century they came to the brine baths - or saltwells - which give the wood its name.

This was the most important spa in the west midlands. Its waters were said to cure all ills - an unlikely assertion, but one with sufficient credibility to ensure a steady stream of customers for hot and cold baths at the Saltwells Inn. Not everyone came to take the waters. The meadows around about were used for Sunday school parties, and in the spring for mayings - the making of daisychains and cowslip balls. The first Sunday in May was the day of "Saltwells Wake" when people would come to enjoy the woodland at its best.

Once in the middle of a vast forest stretching from Cannock to the Wyre this area gave 17th. century environmentalists cause for concern. The growing trade of iron making, with furnaces fuelled by timber, together with the charcoal and shipbuilding trades, was exhausting the woodlands to such an extent that iron masters were losing trade for lack of fuel. Local men, including members of the Earl of Dudley's family who owned a lot of land in the area, developed the use of pit coal as an alternative. The abundance of coal beneath their feet led to the sinking of many mine shafts. When a couple of these flooded it was discovered that there was a lot of salt in the water. Early efforts to recover this by evaporation proved uneconomic, but eventually it was realised that the water itself could be used for medicinal baths.

As well as coal, timber, and salt, fireclay is also present. The famous ceramics company Royal Doulton were responsible for the excavation of what is now Doulton's Claypit. Clay extraction ceased in the 1940's, since when the sides of the old pit have been colonised by a succession of wild plants. Most prominent now are hawthorn, birch, and oak. Also striking are the exposed rocks and shales of the sheer faces within the pit. These are noteworthy enough for the claypit to be designated as a Site of Special Scientific Interest.

Despite, and in some cases because of, the varied land uses over the centuries Saltwells Wood and Doulton's Claypit are home to a wide variety of wildlife. The mature trees in the wood today are about two hundred years old. They are mainly oak, beech, and sycamore. Many younger trees will be seen which have been planted in the last ten years. The long history of woodland cover means that many woodland plants and animals are still present. In spring bluebells carpet the ground, jays and woodpeckers swoop around the canopy, and much-travelled willow warblers announce their arrival in bursts of song. In midsummer yellow flags wave in the Claypit whilst above them kestrels hover hopefully, and speckled wood and purple hairstreak butterflies perform their aerial ballets amongst the leaves and branches. In addition grass snakes, newts, water voles, and mink live out their lives, virtually under the noses and feet of visitors, but rarely seen. The field centre at the back of Saltwells House contains information and displays about these and other denizens of the Reserve.

Saltwells House was built in the 19th. Century by the Earl of Dudley as a tied cottage on the grand scale for the manager of Round Oak Steelworks. This famous Black Country enterprise was about half a mile away. Today it is no more. The place where it stood until the early 1980's is now just another plot within the Dudley Enterprise Zone.

In 1981 the area which includes Saltwells Wood and the Claypit was designated as one of Britain's contributions to the "European Year of Renaissance". This was intended to reflect and realise the potential for nature conservation, recreation, and amenity, in what was then officially "derelict" land. Since that time other areas close by have been brought into the Project. Mushroom Green to the south and Netherton Hill to the north are two such places well worth visiting. The former is a tiny settlement consisting of cottages once occupied by nail-makers and chain-makers. An old chain-making shop is operated there by the Black Country Museum. The quaintly named Mousesweet Brook flows through the hamlet. Netherton Hill's gorse bushes hang beneath Netherton Top Church, looking as if they have done so for many years. This is an illusion as the hill was mined for coal in the 1960's. The landscape today is the result of restoration works in 1973.

Provision for visitors is still being developed in this part of Dudley. The Field Centre will provide up to date information and guidance on exploring and discovering this fascinating area.

# Illey and Lapal

MAP 139 REF. 988/826

Space to park near the houses at the end of Lye Close Lane which is off Carters Lane, at the western end of the Woodgate Valley. These roads can be reached off the A456 Birmingham to Kidderminster road between Quinton and Halesowen. Alternative parking at the Black Horse Public House in Illey Lane.

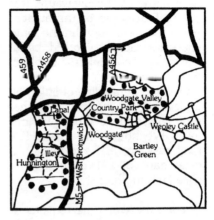

←——— 4.2 miles ———→

*One of the least known and most rural corners of Dudley where the West Midlands County rubs shoulders with Worcestershire. Field paths, rough and muddy in places, with some stiles. Various routes through an historic landscape, along narrow stream valleys, by ancient woods and copses, and with views over the surrounding countryside. Connecting paths to the nearby Woodgate Valley and Waseley Hills Country Parks. Leaflets available from both Dudley and Hereford and Worcestershire Councils. The whole network of paths is way-marked in a most excellent way which should serve as a lesson to all who have responsibility for such things. Credit for this is shared between the local authority, volunteers from the Halesowen Abbey Trust and the Countryside Commission.*

This delightful area gives you a chance to stretch your legs within a stone's throw of the ancient town of Halesowen. The gently ruckled landscape provides every stream with its own miniature ravine, and every little farm with sloping fields. Now mainly down to horsey-culture there is nevertheless a timeless air about the meadows and pastures and the fragments of ancient woodlands.

Walking from Lye Close Lane towards Cooper's Wood you will be walking in the footsteps of the many generations whose business brought them to and from the Abbey, or the market, or the orig-

21

inal Saxon church of St. John the Baptist at Halesowen. So many over so many centuries that today the ancient lanes are lower than the adjoining land, and deserve their name of "hollow-ways". It is a pity that some of the ancient hedgerows are now thrashed into shape instead of being laid, but at least they are mainly still in place. In keeping with the small scale of everything here a line of little pollarded willows line the brook that runs by Cooper's Wood. Further away Wychbury and Clent Hills may be seen. It is said that on a clear day you can even see the Clee Hills in Shropshire.

Beyond the wood the remains of ancient ridge and furrow farming can clearly be seen. At Lowlands Farm a veritable roof garden of mosses and ferns grows on top of a brick lean-to alongside the path. The end of the trunk of a small tree protrudes through the wall beneath this roof, nothing as sophisticated as a beam being needed here. In fact the builder couldn't even be bothered to clear away the previous building because old sandstone blocks support the whole structure.

The delights of the Black Horse Pub may now detain you awhile before you press on to Illey House and Lower Illey Farms. These have neat stables and the ubiquitous lines of Leylandii - as if we had nothing for windbreaks before these and other exotic conifers made their appearance in England. At one point the sunken path is lined by sandstone bound by tangles of gnarled roots. A big

crack willow stands guard over the stream crossing below Lower Illey Farm, and larch and alder somewhat incongruously line the banks behind the farm. In winter the purple-tinged alder catkins suffuse the view with their rich colour. Where the path crosses the next pasture it skirts one of the County's few Sites of Special Scientific Interest - Illey Pastures. These are ancient meadows untainted by plough or chemical spray. In the summer sneezewort and yellow rattle consort with quaking grass, dyer's greenweed, betony and a host of other flowers in all their anachronistic glory.

In stark contrast the path next runs by the Worcestershire Gun Club's land. In an orgy of insensitivity the members of this organisation scatter smithereens of bright orange clays over the woods, the paths, and even into the stream. The latter tries to look attractive as it runs between wooded banks, but pottery shards add nothing to its prospect. If you want to follow the path to Illey Brook Farm be careful here. The Gun Club have a small shack beneath an oak and a crab apple tree - go past this and then turn along the stream so that the water is on your left. This is Illey Brook - said to be home to brown trout, bullhead, dipper and kingfisher. The unusual moschatel (which is a flower not a wine) grows in the wooded strip along the brook's banks. This greeny yellow flower is sometimes called "town-hall clock" because the square stem has a flower on each side.

Whether you take the path to Illey Mill or go past the farm you will have a fairly unpleasant walk for a few hundred yards along Illey Lane before you pick up the path towards the Abbey. There is no footpath at all in parts and the road is usually quite busy.

When you turn off the lane extensive views open up again. Watch for the sharp turn in the open field - the footpath follows old field boundaries which no longer exist! It is possible to get quite close to the ruins of Halesowen Abbey, but they are only open to visitors on a few days each year.

This was an important ecclesiastical house in medieval times, having been founded in 1215. Today the ruins form part of the Manor Abbey Farm buildings in a curious amalgam which does nothing for the architecture of either partner. Walking away from the Abbey to the east great hollows are traversed. These are thought to be the remains of monastic fish ponds. Turning south again at Lapal Lane South a slight rise is crested. This affords a good view of the town of Halesowen with its fine church spire, before you pick your way back to the parking place.

# Woodgate Valley Country Park   | ⊕

## MAP 139 REF. 995/830

A large area of countryside about five miles west of Birmingham City centre, close to Bartley Green and Quinton. Car park and Visitors' Centre in Clapgate Lane near to Junction 3 of the M5 (although access from this junction is not direct). Clapgate Lane is one of the roads linking the A458 at Quinton to the B4127 between Harborne and Northfield.

*About 450 acres following the course of the Bourne Brook containing a wide variety of habitats; woodland, wetland and hay meadows. Owned by Birmingham City Council, and managed by rangers. Walking is generally easy, with good paths on shallow gradients. An urban farm situated close to the Visitor Centre is open to visitors. There is a varied programme of events - including guided walks - throughout the year. Good facilities for the disabled. Refreshments and toilets.*

Woodgate Valley Country Park is one of the success stories of urban conservation in the 1980's. Its peaceful fields and hedgerows link the Worcestershire countryside in the west to the leafy suburbs of Edgbaston and Harborne in the east. Although some housing intrudes into the valley from Clapgate Lane you may still enjoy a rural atmosphere here. And yet it was so nearly ruined by facto-

23

ries which were planned for the Clapgate Lane area. Thanks to the efforts of local residents, assisted by conservation bodies like the Urban Wildlife Trust, the proposals were rejected. Better still - with that rejection came plans for proper management of the valley by making it a country park. That was in 1984, and in 1987 the purpose built Visitor Centre was opened. One of the objectives of the City Council is to demonstrate conservation management of the open grassland and woodlands.

Woodgate Valley is one of those valleys named for the locality they are found in rather than the watercourse which runs through them. In this case the stream is the Bourn Brook. As the word 'bourn' (or 'bourne') is derived from the Old English 'burna' meaning 'stream' it is likely that this trickle of water has been bubbling along here for many centuries. This being so you may pause to wonder why its course is not more rich in water loving plants, and why the bourn itself does not spill lazily over the adjoining meadows from time to time. Alas this poor brook has been subjected to the modern mania for so-called improvement. Done sensitively of course this need not be a disaster. The Bourn Brook was treated somewhat insensitively however. In 1973 almost the whole stretch from Watery Lane in the west to Harborne Lane in the east was dealt with at once, resulting in the destruction of much of the natural vegetation. Hopefully this will gradually return, especially if it is assisted by the current managers. In the meantime centuries of evolution have been wiped out. Even so a pleasant walk may still be enjoyed along the banks.

Long before the legalised vandalism of the 1970's some of the really ancient denizens of the valley had already gone. When we may wonder did beavers disappear? Were they still around when Roger de Somery rebuilt the nearby Weoley Castle at the end of the 13th. century? Did the presence of wild boar in this part of what would then have been Worcestershire influence a later owner of the castle - William Berkeley - to support Richard III at Bosworth in 1485? (The boar was Richard's emblem).

Birmingham is very short of historical buildings, each century's architecture serving merely to provide the rubble upon which the next century's developments were founded. What little there is left of Weoley Castle can be seen in nearby Alwood Rd. close to California to the east of Woodgate Valley. The 'castle' was a large moated manor house. Its remains - mainly thick sandstone walls between one and three feet high - have been exposed and are open for inspection from March to October between 2pm and 5pm Tuesday to Friday. There is also a small museum on the site. The name Weoley is derived from the Saxon ''weoh-leah' meaning a wood or clearing containing a heathen temple. It would appear therefore that the site was of some importance long before the

Norman conquest.

You may be surprised to find California in Birmingham (although as it happens there are a number of Hollywoods around). There is no romantic tale of a pioneer from hereabouts working his way to the west coast of America and naming the sunshine state after his fondly remembered home. It was the reverse which happened. Isaac Flavell was one of the thousands of people who flocked to California in the 1840's - a genuine '49er -. Unlike most of those people he did make his fortune and, returning to Woodgate, bought Stonehouse Farm and called the area California.

Isaac Flavell was partly responsible for the industrial activity which interrupted hundreds of years of agriculture in the valley. His chosen spot at Stonehouse Farm was very close to a canal which was built in 1790. Where this canal crossed the valley itself it was put into a deep tunnel beneath the fields. The mounds of spoil resulting from this excavation can be clearly seen across Woodgate Valley today. Mr. Flavell dug clay out of his land and had a brickworks on the site. He made good use of the canal, using it to bring coal in to heat his kilns, and to take the finished bricks out to the expanding towns of the Black Country. He must have thought even this too dear a way to operate because eventually he tried to mine coal in the valley as well, the remains of his slag heap still being apparent near to Bartley Green Girls' School.

The clay also provided the raw material for another local trade - pottery. At one time all of the local nurseries were supplied with their earthenware pots by the pottery in California. All of these things have come and gone. Today the valley is green and peaceful again, as it would once always have been. The kestrel hovering hopefully, waiting for lunch to scuttle into view, the song thrush serenading the morning star, the busy pipistrelle bats patrolling the tree tops at dawn and dusk, know nothing of Mr. Flavell, or the pottery, or the castle ruins. They are part of the timelessness of nature, they are living links with an ancient past and a distant future. They will enliven your walk, as will a hundred different wild flowers, a dozen or more songbirds, the old hedgerows with their wild roses cascading over the paths and the acres of grass waving in the wind. If you wish to explore further afield there are footpaths leading out of the valley into the surrounding area.

You may walk across the old fields, no longer distinguishable, but whose names echo the old ways, names like Pigsty Field, Middle Leasow, Ox Leasow, Barn Piece and First Meadow Piece. The old farms too have had their day - Stonehouse Farm, Wilderness Farm (was there a time when the valley was thought of as a wilderness?) Four Dwellings Farm and Nonsuch Farm. Nonsuch Farm? Ah yes, that name is said to date back to the Civil War when Oliver Cromwell is supposed to have hidden in a barn. When royalists came looking for him they were told 'None such man is here'... However you decide to spend your time in the Woodgate Valley you will be able to reflect upon the survival of these splendid rural landscapes in such an urban area.

# Park Lime Pits

MAP 139 REF. 032/002

**Car parking at the Manor Arms in Park Road, off the B4154 which connects the A461 and A454 roads about one mile north-east of Walsall town centre.**

*Easy walking in a small area remarkable both for the unspoilt nature of its landscape, and for the fact that such attractiveness lies so close to Walsall town centre. Rough paths, with stiles and steps, in gently undulating countryside. This is a local nature reserve managed by Walsall Council and there is a ranger service on site.*

This small patch of what was once Staffordshire countryside holds a wealth of local and natural history. Its limestone has been used for many purposes by scores of generations of people, Rushall Hall was an important house during the Civil War and the Manor Arms claims to be Britain's oldest pub. The hedgerows in the fields are full of guelder rose and meadowsweet holds sweet sway in the hayfields. Lobster-like freshwater crayfish lurk in the canal and in the flooded lime pits.

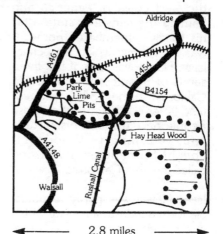

2.8 miles

A walk from the Manor Arms to the south along the canal towpath takes you into the small fields of the local farms. Moorhen and mallard cluck scoldingly at each other, and at the cattle peacefully grazing by the still water. The tow path is part of the Beacon Way which continues to Hayhead and Cuckoo's Nook (an area described elswhere in this book).

Walking from the Manor Arms south west towards the lime pits you are presented with an almost medieval landscape (provided that a train is not in sight!). The fields roll softly up to the white walls of the churchyard. The spire of the church of Saint Michael's rises elegantly over all as if reaching up

26

to the larks, whose songs cascade back down to earth as they have ever since the primeval forest was cleared.

The lime pits themselves have been abandoned for over 100 years. Their limpid waters - often with the blue tinge that gave them the local name of "blue holes" - are deep and dangerous to people. They are though ideal for the many fishes, dragonflies and caddisflies which thrive in the clean water. You can sit on the bank of one of the pits munching your own lunch, whilst watching fish munch theirs after choosing from the aerial buffet of insects alighting on the surface of the water. One of the pits has a stand of true bulrush. This has thin dark green stems, an altogether more delicate plant than the brutish reedmace which has usurped its name. Nearby the much rarer lesser reedmace grows.

The presence of limestone in the locality has had a major influence on the town of Walsall. The midlands is not generally thought of as a limestone area, but there was sufficient beneath ground to serve the iron smelters of the Industrial Revolution. There are two places in particular where the limestone is apparent at the surface: Dudley (especially at Castle Hill, Mons Hill and the Wren's Nest) and this part of Walsall where the outcrops are more low-lying. For centuries limestone was quarried here for agriculture and for building. The white walls of the churchyard wall remain as testimony to the latter. Then came

the discovery that limestone was useful in the smelting of iron, and the growth of the metal industry.

The final piece of the Walsall jigsaw is the use of limestone in tanning leather. The leather industry is now an important part of the local economy. It has not been so important for as long as many people think. Originally Walsall was a centre for the metal fittings - such as buckles - associated with leather harnesses, belts and so on. As late as the Crimean War these metal fittings were the primary trade of the area and the leather work was still secondary. From about the beginning of the 20th. Century the balance changed. Walsall Football Club may therefore be justifiably nicknamed "the Saddlers". Although the town's workshops have often produced the ball used in the F.A. Cup Final the town's team has yet to appear in one of the matches.

For a long time the fields around Park Lime Pits provided everything the leather workers needed: the limestone mentioned above, bark from oak and chestnut trees from which they extracted the tannin which gives the process of tanning its name, and hides from the cattle which grazed the lush vegetation. Now everything has to be transported from much further away - many of the hides for example are imported.

Rushall Hall is tucked discreetly behind the church as if the excitements of its past have been enough for it, and that it now wishes to rest in peace. Its owner is certainly very security conscious, having installed notices making it clear that this is private property, and cameras to watch the gates. A sign on the main gate shows that inflation never used to be a problem. It says "Any person who omits to shut and fasten this gate is liable to a penalty not exceeding forty shillings." It is cast in iron and so was obviously meant to be there a long time.

The hall was known as Rushall Castle when the Harpur family first built it in the 14th. Century. They supported the House of Lancaster in the Wars of the Roses. The Civil War saw the Leigh family in residence. They were Parliamentarians who were forced to defend the Hall against Prince Rupert himself. Another Walsall family - the Lanes of Bentley Hall - were Royalists. When the Hall was captured Colonel Lane was installed as the garrison's commander.

The reason for all this interest in Rushall Hall was that the main route from London to the North West passed between Rushall and Tamworth, and Tamworth was also held for the Crown. (Now of course the road - the M6 motorway - passes further to the west, although the main railway line still runs through the Trent Valley at Lichfield and Tamworth). The situation was so serious for Cromwell's allies that they had to caution the merchants of Manchester about sending goods south until they had secured the route again. Accordingly no less than 6000 soldiers were sent to deal with the 200 Royalists encamped at Rushall. These overwhelming odds no doubt contributed to the Hall surrendering to Parliamentary control with only two fatalities amongst the belligerents.

There is then plenty for the walker to experience and to ponder upon whilst strolling back to the Manor Arms. Make sure to visit this old inn. The present building is not the first to have occupied the site, but it is one of Walsall's oldest buildings. Its claim to be the oldest licensed premises in Britain may or may not be true, but it does possess a charm lacking in the synthetic "olde worlde" pubs of today. It is short of something that almost all other pubs have - a bar of any sort. Drinks are served with no barrier between you and the host.

# Hay Head Wood

MAP 139 REF. 041/991

**Two miles east of Walsall town centre. On Longwood Lane leading south from A454 Walsall / Aldridge road at canal bridge. Car park.**

*13 acres of woodland belonging to & managed by Walsall Council. Some of the paths rough & muddy in the winter, with steps on steep slopes in a few places. The Beacon Way passes through Hay Head.*

This attractive woodland is typical of many sites in and around built up areas. It has every appearance of being natural but has in fact seen many different sorts of land use, mainly associated with local industry. In the case of Hay Head these have included the mining and burning of lime, coppicing of some of the shrubs and trees, the building of a canal and winding hole, and even a small airfield.

Lime was used in blast furnaces and its presence in Walsall and Dudley helped to ensure the success of local iron masters during the Industrial Revolution. Hay Head lime was used for building materials as well. In the early 19th Century advertisements for "Brindley's British Cement" included the claim "prepared exclusively from Hay Head Waterproof Lime". The last lime was extracted about 1870 although as late as 1921 the Birmingham Canal Navigation Company were taking clay from the site to repair their canals.

To make transporting the lime easier a short canal arm was built from the Rushall Canal, which is still in existence, just across the fields on the opposite side of Longwood Lane. This arm was a watery cul-de-sac and so it had to be opened out into a small basin to enable the boats to turn round. Such turning places are called "winding holes".

The woodland has now had the best part of 70 years to develop, and nature has taken full advantage. Walk just a few yards from the car park and you will be enveloped in trees, with perhaps a moorhen for company as it clucks its way over the waters of the old canal. The lime rich soil favours both ash and guelder rose, the latter being very common in the hedgerows between Hay Head and Park Lime Pits (covered elsewhere in this book). Another lime loving plant which may be found in the more open grassy areas is kidney vetch. This is a low growing member of the pea family with bright yellow, red, or orange flower heads. It used to be a medicinal herb, a preparation made from it being used to treat wounds.

The remains of lime burning pits, pump housings, and pit shafts will be encountered in various places. In the peace of the woodlands today it is difficult to imagine the sights, sounds, and smells of 150 years ago: little trucks full of lime-stone being shuttled back and forth, narrow boats turning in the basin, the clamour of the steam pumps drawing water out of the pits, the smell of coal and lime burning together for up to a week at a time to produce quicklime. In their places now may be the shrill scolding of a wren, the harsh call of a jay, the brilliant red berries of the guelder rose, and the strong smell of ramsons (wild garlic). Somehow some ancient wood-land plants have survived here such as bluebells, wood anenome, and wood sorrel.

Amongst the many different trees to be found is the aspen. This is a small and somewhat delicate member of the willow and poplar family. Its scientific name - Popu-lus tremula - refers to the way it seems to tremble in the slightest breeze. The reason for this trembling is apparent if you run the stems of the leaves through your fingers. They are flattened from side to side rather then rounded or square as in most other plants. This means that the slightest pres-sure on the leaf, such as the mer-est whisper of wind, is enough to make it move. The flattened peti-oles also make it very easy to identify aspens amongst other trees. In the autumn the leaves turn bright yellow.

*Guelder Rose, in fact not a rose at all*

30

There are a number of paths running through Hay Head, and a short guide is available from the library in Walsall. You can walk through the woods into two further pieces of woodland - the Dingle & Cuckoos Nook - following the Beacon Way to its eponymous landmark Barr Beacon.

When you do return to the car park consider for a moment the large field in front of the car park. This, believe it or not, used to be Walsall Airport. Presumably only light aircraft used it, as the thought of anything else landing or taking off is daunting. One advantage of having been an airstrip is that the grass has escaped the worst ravages of modern agriculture. This means that there is a wonderful show of wild flowers in the summer. Meadow buttercups, meadow vetchling, and red and white clover, to name just a few, attract many different sorts of insects. Amongst these may be seen common blues which lay their eggs on low growing members of the pea family, especially birds-foot trefoil.

# Rough Wood

## MAP 139 REF. 981/009

Car park with picnic tables in Hunts Lane in the Short Heath area one and a half miles north-west of Walsall. Hunts Lane is off Bloxwich Road North, which in turn is off the A462 road from Willenhall to New Invention north of Willenhall.

*80 acres (200 hectares) of oak woodland managed as a local nature reserve by Walsall Council. Part of a larger area - 346 acres (830 hectares) - of urban fringe land designated as a country park. A network of muddy, sometimes narrow, paths guide the visitor through the woods and around small pools and wetland. Leaflet describing a nature trail available from Walsall Council.*

Houses, a motorway and a canal may seem to offer an unlikely setting for the gem that is Rough Wood. Perhaps though their proximity serves to highlight the glories of the woodland in a way that a more rural scene would not. Whether it be from the carpets of bluebells in the spring, the many coloured autumn leaves, or the white tracery of frost rinded branches in deepest winter, the walker is assured of a worthwhile

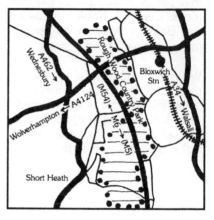

◄———— 2.8 miles ————►

welcome. From the small car park, with its remarkably informative notice board, a variety of routes can be taken.

Today's visitors are the latest in a long line of people to enjoy Rough Wood. The mighty oaks standing sentinel-like in the glades have seen many changes. Even before these oaks were acorns the area was high forest. In the 12th. Century this was all part of Cannock Forest, a royal hunting ground where deer and wild boar roamed free - and heaven help any peasant who stocked his own table with the King's beasts. At some point the King must have grown tired of this part of his estate. About 400 years ago the animals were all killed and the forest was felled. The timber was used to fuel the furnaces of the Black Country. For a couple of hundred

32

years the area was left to its own devices. Then in the 1700's the Industrial Revolution brought a demand for coal. Beneath Rough Wood there was plenty of this and very soon it was being mined. The Wyrley and Essington Canal which still runs around the edge of the wood was built to transport this and other materials (such as limestone) to the towns of the Black Country. The coal was needed to fuel the furnaces of the rapidly expanding metal industry. There was plenty of this in Walsall but in addition it became a centre for leather making. One of the requirements of this trade is tannin, often obtained from oak bark. No doubt the oaks of Rough Wood made their contribution to the development of this activity. Despite all of the upheavals enough of the wood survived for us to be able to say that there has been a continuous history of woodland here. The value of this should not be understated. Small as it is Rough Wood comprises about one tenth of all of the oak woodland in the West Midlands County.

As well as the oaks for which the wood is best known there are plenty of other trees and shrubs here. Shimmering aspens, elders replete with luscious black berries, occasional crab apples, rowan, alder buckthorns, birch and sweet chestnut trees may each take the eye. Scarlet hips on the wild roses help to identify them in the autumn - oval hips on dog roses and round hips on field roses. There are plenty of dog roses and many of them have red cotton wool-like growths in addition to the hips.

These are bedeguar galls. Inside each are several dozen tiny grubs. They have hatched from eggs laid by an insignificant parasitic wasp (Diplolepis rosae). The galls form when the grubs emerge from the eggs. Each grub is in its own little cell, eating away at the plant tissue from the inside. When full grown the grubs pupate, turn into adult wasps, bite their way out of the gall and begin the whole process over again. Many other galls appear on other plants, especially oak trees.

The wetland in Rough Wood includes some small pools, the canal, and a silted up wharf which is now a marsh dominated by reedmace. The nearby bridge over the canal is a real monstrosity. When first built it was twice as wide as it is now. It may have been no more handsome for that but at least it would have been in proportion.

Fortunately you can turn away from the bridge into the wood and enjoy the speckled wood butterflies dancing in the dappled light, or the flash of white as a jay jinks through the tree tops. As you move deeper into the wood it is easy to forget that it is an isolated fragment. There is a genuine woodland atmosphere. Gnarled trunks, twisted branches, toadstools the size of dinner plates and old coppice stools provide a timeless backdrop to your walk. The woodland floor reveals past land-use. In one part of the wood old spoil heaps rise above head height (although they are now clothed in trees and other plants) in another the ground has many shallow depressions where local people dug surface coal out. Close to the car park what may be a centuries old bank and ditch could mark the ancient boundary of the wood.

The rest of the country park is like young wine of doubtful vintage. It may or may not mature into something worthwhile, but for now it is best left alone. Some of the land is laid out for amenity and has a peculiarly sterile character, especially around Sneyd Reservoir. The rest is immature landscape typical of recently re-claimed industrial land. Pockets of it have their charm, but there is still too much intrusion from our society's less attractive pursuits to recommend it for a quiet walk.

# Sandwell Valley ⊕

**MAP 139 REF. 029/927**

**Car park at Forge Mill Farm in Forge Lane which connects the A41 West Bromwich to Birmingham Road with Newton Rd. (the A4041 West Bromwich to Great Barr road). Three other car parks available in Forge Lane.**

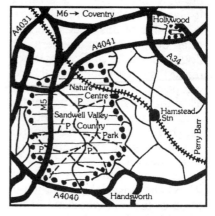

◄──── 3.2 miles ────►

*This is a large area (about 2000 acres) of encapsu-lated countryside between West Bromwich, Walsall and Birmingham. The River Tame wends its way through pastures grazed by horses and cattle. Working farms rub shoulders with golf courses and open grassland. Woods, pools and streams fed by pure springs complete the land-scape kaleidoscope which stops only about five miles from the centre of Birming-ham. Part of the area is a country park run by Sandwell Council. A net-work of well made paths* *enable the visitor to gain easy access to all parts of the valley, although some parts may be very wet even in the summer. Plenty of refreshment points and toi-lets.*

The Sandwell Valley offers a re-markable variety of wildlife, scenery and attractions for a place firmly rooted in an industrial area. Sandwell Council actually has a milk quota for its herd of Jersey cows, which enjoy the benefits of a modern dairy unit at Forge Mill Farm. This is a demonstration farm for local schoolchildren. In contrast the Council manages a farm on the other side of the valley in the way it would have been run in late Victorian times. The Royal Society for the Protection of Birds (RSPB) has a reserve and nature centre on the opposite side of Forge Mill Lake to the car park. Away from these "honeypots" there are plenty of quiet places and plenty of good walking country.

One of the main features of the valley is water. Numerous springs, especially on the southern side, provide an endless supply of clean sparkling water. This gurgles its way along streams and through lots of little pools as it makes its way to the river. Two large pools - Swan Pool and Forge Mill Pool - provide homes for numerous waterfowl as well as facilities for water sports. The flock of wintering waterfowl on Forge Mill Pool attracts many birdwatchers. The River Tame itself suffers from passing through areas dominated by industry before it reaches the valley, but it is cleaner now than it has been since before the Industrial Revolution. Kingfishers and little grebe may both be seen prospecting for fish, which is a very good sign that the water has improved.

The Tame is a tributary of the Trent and for thousands of years migrating birds have used it as a flyway. The RSPB reserve near to Hamstead (which is also a Local Nature Reserve) is amongst their 20 best reserves in the country - both for the variety of birds and for the number of visitors. It gives the lie to those who maintain that wildlife and people do not mix, and that the two should be kept apart for conservation to be effective. The reserve is managed in a way that allows people to get very close to even shy birds, such as waders, without disturbing them. Depending on the time of the year you may enjoy the exuberant songs of larks, the quiet elegance of redshank or sandpiper, or the gentle chuckles of the ducks as they settle down to roost in a winter dusk.

The RSPB reserve with its carefully managed marshes and pools, all created - together with Forge Mill Pool - in the last 15 years, is something of an irony. On the opposite side of Forge Lane to the car park is Swan Pool. This is an ancient piece of water which had the misfortune to be close to the Jubilee Colliery, the remains of which are now used as a boat store. It lay neglected amongst the ruins of the pit until the 1970's. The wildlife did not mind the dereliction too much. Reed buntings nested in the reedmace beds, toads bred in the margins of the pool, and huge swan mussels lay in its mud. As part of improving the area for amenity the pool was drained and enlarged. The marsh and carr around its margins went, the reed buntings were evicted (although they are still in the valley) and a bland landscape was created where before diversity delighted those who could see beyond the ruins of the mine. The engineer taketh away and the engineer giveth back...

Doing your best to ignore the M6 motorway which runs through the valley you may wander past Swan Pool, to the woods and pools which are on land which was once typical 18th. century parkland. The Earls of Dartmouth lived here until the end of the 19th. century, successors to the monks of Sandwell Priory, who in turn followed the presumably lone inhabitant of a hermitage. Deer roamed parkland pastures punctuated by fine oak and sweet chestnut trees. An avenue of the latter species led to the front doors of a large but undistinguished mansion - Sandwell Hall. The remains of the avenue of sweet chestnuts may be seen in the woods near to Sandwell Park Golf Course where their massive stunted boles lurk within the younger oak and birch.

The site of the Hall and Priory has been excavated and lies alongside the main path to Park Farm. An ancient well fed by one of the springs is reputed to be the site of the hermitage. This has been restored to its Victorian "splendour" which, whilst historically accurate, is completely out of character with its setting. When the priory was dissolved it is said that Thomas Cromwell (Cardinal Wolsey's hit-man) came here himself to finalise the accounts. The money was said to have formed part of the endowment of Cardinal's College Oxford - what is now Christ's College.

Walking over the motorway brings you to Park Farm. This is a most remarkable building. Completed in about 1702 it consists of an open-fronted barn (the openings are now glazed) and a square farmyard with small towers at each corner. Within the farmyard are animal pens, an old dairy and a dovecote. A cafe provides welcome refreshment. The upper floor has been converted to meeting rooms for school groups and others studying the locality. A charge is made for entry on some days. Within this complex there is a shop and exhibitions depicting bygone days in the valley. Of particular interest is the exhibition about the priory.

If you walk back to over the motorway and to the other side of Forge Lane you will arrive at the highest point in the valley, appropriately called Hill Top. Here Birmingham City centre is just under five miles away, and the tide of houses in Handsworth wash along the edge of the valley. Standing amongst the concrete remains of war time gun emplacements reminds us of recent history, when the peace of the area was shattered daily. Now that peace has returned and everyone can enjoy the flowers, birdsong and quiet waters of this remarkable countryside enclave. And it is all downhill to your car at Forge Mill Farm.

# Hollywood Community Nature Park ⊕

## MAP 139 REF. 051/944

**No car park, but space available in Whitecrest. off Queslett Rd. half-a-mile east of the Scott Arms (the junction of the A34 - Birmingham / Walsall road - and the A4041 - the West Bromwich / Sutton road).**

*A fragment of oak / birch woodland which once formed part of the Scott Estate at St. Margarets. It is now owned by Sandwell Council. Twisting paths and undulating ground create a feeling of space and peace within a relatively small area. Local residents and the Urban Wildlife Trust have carried out management work in recent years.*

This tiny piece of woodland survives amongst the paraphernalia of suburbia. It stands both as a reminder of the wider landscape which once held sway here, and as a testament to the resilience of nature. Despite its isolation from the rest of the St. Margarets Estate (now lying on the other side of the M6 motorway) and the nearby houses, shops and schools, Hollywood has kept a lot of woodland plants and animals. The carpets of bluebells in May, so typical of English woodlands but so rare elsewhere in the

world, are a joy to see. Woodland birds like great tits, jays and chiffchaff may still be seen and heard. In the autumn fruits, seeds, nuts and toadstools litter the leafy floor as they have done for hundreds of years. Everything may have changed around the wood but nature goes on in her timeless way, defying our efforts to control and sanitise our suburban habitat.

Wandering through Hollywood is rewarding at any time of the year. Springtime is of course the glorious season in woodlands. In the spring the woodland floor is carpeted with flowers and birdsong fills the air. Come the long hot days of summer and the shade of the canopy offers cooling relief, whilst the quiet buzz of insects replaces the more musical birdsong. In autumn the wet woodland glistens and glows gold and yellow as long shafts of sunlight pierce the once impenetrable canopy. In one place a web of gossamer catches the rays, in another a late flying speckled wood butterfly basks in the warm spotlight. And in the winter frost crispens everything. It hardens the paths, turns leaves and branches into delicate filigree, and seems to sweeten the air you breathe.

Woodlands are shy of revealing their secrets. Any one visit will allow but a glimpse of the wildlife to be seen. Every hour of the day and night different insects, birds or flowers will be apparent. In Hollywood at midnight common quakers, lesser swallow prominents and lunar marbled browns flit amongst the trees. These are just a few of the many moths which live in or visit the wood. They are somewhat less spectacular to look at than their names might suggest; that matters not one iota to the bats which patrol the wood hoping that supper too is on the wing.

This Hollywood may not be as famous as its Californian counterpart but it has its own array of star performers. The performance is continuous - 24 hours a day, seven days a week, 52 weeks of the year. No tickets needed.

# Sutton Park

MAP 139 REF. 090/955

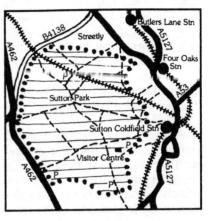

3.4 miles

Banners Gate entrance to the park is on the A452 (Chester Rd) 11/2 miles west of Sutton Coldfield town centre. Almost entirely an SSSI. Car parks, toilets and refreshment facilities in various places within the park.

*To visit Sutton Park is to experience a unique place. Its 2500 acres contain lowland heathland, ancient woodland and rare wetlands. Metalled roads, well surfaced tracks and a network of footpaths make most of the park easily accessible. Despite this it is very easy to find solitude, and even enjoy a sense of wilderness, in an amazingly unspoilt landscape. Sutton Park is the jewel in the countryside of the west midlands. It has never been cultivated or agriculturally improved. Over 400 different flowers grow within its confines, its woodlands are the finest of their type (oak / holly / rowan) outside the New Forest, and its pools, streams and bogs contain many rare plants.*

As this book is about walking in both the County of West Midlands and in Warwickshire it is fitting

that the most exciting place covered should have an identity crisis about these counties. When local government was re-organised in 1974 the Royal Borough of Sutton Coldfield, together with its famous park, was incorporated into the City of Birmingham. This meant that the town and the park left Warwickshire and became part of the County of West Midlands. Since then controversy has raged about the wisdom of this move, and about whether or not Sutton will remain in the new county or return to Warwickshire.

Suttonians are rightly proud and fiercely defensive of "their" park. They have good reason. Since the time of the kings of Mercia (and perhaps for centuries before) the area has been used for recreation. Alternatively a forest or a chase, depending on whether the Crown

39

or a local noble owned the land, the park was given to the townspeople in perpetuity by Henry VIII. This was due to the influence of Bishop Vesey, Bishop of Exeter. A local boy made good he was a friend of the King (presumably it would have been bad for his career if he had been the King's enemy!) and an even bigger friend of his home town. Henry himself is reputed to have hunted wild boar in the park.

The result of this royal patronage, ancient use as a hunting ground and centuries of care by the burghers of Sutton, is a place which could not have been designed (as landscaped parks were designed in the 18th century). It was left largely unscathed by the Enclosures, and engenders a powerful sense of place which is apparent to all who visit it. Historically and culturally it is as significant as the nearby Lichfield Cathedral, or the victorian architecture of the city centre just a few miles away. The landscape, flora and fauna are typical of that which once thrived throughout the region. Buildings and farms may have all but obliterated this elsewhere; in Sutton Park you can experience living history as you gaze on views that would have been familiar to medieval peasant, Saxon warlord and Roman soldier alike.

Tudor Rose

40

The first thing to do when you arrive in the park is to divest yourself of your car as quickly as possible. The car park just inside Banners Gate is handily placed for you to explore the Longmoor Valley which stretches away to the north, or Westwood Coppice which runs around the perimeter fence from the car park. This is not the best piece of woodland in the park, being more open and even-aged in character than the woods of Holly Hurst or the Gumslade. If you have plenty of time to spare then it is quite feasible to walk around the edge of the park - a distance of about eight miles. If you do so then you will find yourself on Ryknield Street soon after leaving Westwood Coppice. This is a Roman road and one of only a handful of scheduled ancient monuments in Birmingham. The legions may well have camped on Rowton's Hill, and refreshed themselves at the spring bubbling out of Rowton's Well. The military have returned again and again to the park. The bowmen of Agincourt trained here, & in the First World War wounded soldiers convalesced here.

A camp of a different sort was set up in 1957. From the 1st. to the 12th. of August the park played host to the World Scout Jamboree. The event is commemorated by a small stone obelisk in the middle of the park. It's inscription informs you that 32,000 scouts from 87 parts of the world took part in the jamboree, and that they were visited by the Queen. Although only lasting for 13 days it is claimed that irreversible damage was caused by this monster camp. For instance nightjars are reputed to have left with the scouts and have never returned. The camp was on the open grassland to the north-west of the stone.

This area was used for agriculture during the war and was already degraded before the jamboree. It is one of the few places within the park which looks (and is) botanically poor. Even so it serves as a playground for countless families on summer afternoons. The woodland edge of this area contains a number of crab-apple trees. These are most easily spotted in the early winter when the short dark trees stand like moody guardians over their spilled crop of bright green little apples.

This part of the park is accessible by car only through Streetly Gate (MAP 139 REF. 088/986). There are a number of places to park in and around Streetly Wood, but please do use the proper car parks.

The finest area of the park is the northern corner between the railway line and Four Oaks. Even though the marsh fritillary butterflies no longer flit over the devil's-bit scabious and lesser spearwort, other insects - such as emperor moths, speckled wood butterflies and hawker dragonflies - birds - including jays and green woodpeckers - and a host of flowers await the explorer. Bracebridge and Little Bracebridge pools lie calm beneath open skies. The latter is fringed with bog bean and

41

yellow flag which often conceal a skulking heron. In most of this area it is possible to enjoy deceptively wide views without any sign of humanity in them. Not a building, fence, hedge, post or pylon offends the eye.

If you walk around Bracebridge Pool your reward will be a beautiful view over the lake, complete with a perfectly placed little island. Bobby Brown's Restaurant does not really cater for walkers, although if you are lucky the refreshment kiosk nearby will be open. This is a traditional watering hole, Bobby Brown's standing on the site of a Tudor hunting lodge. Who knows but that Henry VIII stood here supping mead whilst Bishop Vesey sold him the idea of protecting the park by giving it to the local people - an early conservationist in action. On a more recent note locals still recall with regretful wistfulness the fisherman's breakfasts provided by the hostelry which immediately preceded Bobby Brown's, and which did cater for walkers.

There is far more to Sutton Park than can be encompassed here. A number of books are available in Sutton which give more details. I will finish with a couple of things. On the Wyndley side of the park a group of pine trees adorns the top of a small rise. They are reputed to mark the centre of England. Unfortunately so do a number of other places in this part of the country - including the cyclists' memorial in Meriden! Finally - whether you are enjoying a long brisk walk or a gentle stroll you may pause to reflect that the fact that the park has survived centuries of change in the landscape all around it is something of a miracle. A miracle the results of which are ours to enjoy, and to pass on to future generations.

# River Cole (Project Kingfisher) | ⊕

**MAP 139 REF. 144/884**

Car park at or near the Cole Hall Farm (a public house) in Cole Hall Lane, Kitts Green. This is near to the mid-point of over seven miles of riverside footpaths which start at the A45 (Coventry Road) in Small Heath and finish at Chelmsley Wood. Walking along the river provides a combination of suburban sights and sounds with those of the countryside.

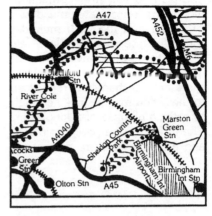

◄——————— 5.4 miles ———————►

*The River Cole in east Birmingham has a countryside management scheme called Project Kingfisher. The project is providing footpaths, creating wildlife habitats, organising countryside events and has a ranger service (based at the Norman Chamberlain playing fields). The river threads its way through a broad flat valley far richer in wildlife than its suburban setting indicates. Birmingham City Council publishes a leaflet about the area.*

It is lucky that east Birmingham remained undeveloped for longer than other parts of the City. The mad scramble for building land in the 19th. Century spelt the end for many small rivers like the River Cole. They were re-routed

or buried underground when they were in the way of the builders. In the case of the Cole Valley it was well into the 20th. Century before its land fell prey to Birmingham's expanding population. When it did it became a huge dormitory area, with many houses and relatively few factories. The riverside meadows became playing fields and recreation grounds, with remnants of the hedgerows and coppices of days gone by allowed to remain in unwanted corners.

Today the clock is being turned back. Project Kingfisher aims to manage the valley for recreation and wildlife. Major planting, pool and wetland, footpath and interpretation schemes are returning the Cole to its wildlife, and helping its tens of thousands of new neighbours to understand and enjoy its unique charm.

43

From Cole Hall Lane you can walk upstream towards the City at Small Heath or downstream towards the Solihull border and Chelmsley Wood. Whichever way you go you will find yourself in what were once water meadows. The river and the path meander through these together. In a few places the banks have been cut into miniature cliffs, and where there are overhanging trees close to these you may be lucky enough to catch a glimpse of a kingfisher. The trees provide perching places and the little cliffs are perfect for kingfishers to nest in. They are still breeding here, hence the project's name. In summer tall herbs, such as Himalayan balsam, greater willowherb and meadowsweet, sway gently in the breeze. Butterflies will accompany you - meadow browns and skippers in the long grasses, whites and tortoiseshells around the flowers. Tall poplars and willows crowd in upon the Cole at Stechford. At the opposite end of the walk Yorks Wood remains as the only piece of ancient woodland left in the Valley. Its springtime

Kingfisher

bluebells and summer warblers are reminders of its countryside past, whilst the low flying airliners droning into Birmingham International Airport are reminders that you are still in the city.

At any time of the year birds abound in the valley. The playing fields attract gulls in the winter and migrating wheatears in the spring and autumn. Babbs Mill Lake always has its complement of ducks and geese. Tits, warblers, magpies, linnets, and finches may be seen or heard in and around the trees and scrub. The river itself is a flyway for birds, such as waders, on their migration flights. It is a tributary of the River Trent and the birds fly along the valley today just as they have always done. You may see redshank or common sandpiper wheeling between the banks, or resting and feeding at the water's edge. At Cole Hall Farm snipe lie up in the marshy areas, waiting until you are about to tread on them before they explode into flight almost in your face.

Finally a little curiosity. Anyone who has driven into Birmingham along the M6 motorway will have seen "E II R" cut into a grassy bank on the left just before the City boundary. You can walk up to this feature from the river. It is Solihull Council's homage to the Sovereign and has been maintained for several years. There is a nice patch of bird's-foot trefoil in the middle of the "R".

# Sheldon Country Park                    ⊕

**MAP 139 REF. 152/845**

**Car park by St. Giles church-
yard off Church Rd. Sheldon,
about half-a-mile north of the
A45 Birmingham / Coventry
Rd. The turning off Coventry
Rd. is into Sheaf Lane, which
becomes Church Rd.**

*Sheldon Country Park -
managed by Birmingham
City Council - is sand-
wiched between the houses
of the city and Birmingham
International Airport. Its
fields and hederows mark
the boundary of open countryside on the south-eastern
edge of the city. Comprising
260 acres of open land the
park has good flat paths
which meander across the
old fields and alongside a
small river. Plenty of picnic
places will be found. The
peace and quiet is fre-
quently punctuated by the
sounds of airliners taking
off and landing at the airport next door. For those
who choose to do so it is
possible to stand virtually
at the end of the main run-
way whilst the aeroplanes
pass just a few feet overhead. Toilets and refreshments available at Old Rectory Farm where the Coun-
try Park rangers are based.*

Since farming ceased to be the
main activity here the land has
been used for playing fields and
for a golf course. The latter had

to go when the airport was last
extended in 1981. This could be
some sort of record by virtue of
the fact that the rest of the country now seems to have a mania
for building golf courses, and
there is certainly a demand for facilities in Birmingham. The wide
open spaces of the playing fields
have left a legacy of large and
lonely oaks scattered around the
edges of the park. They contrast
with the young plantations of
trees such as cherry, field maple,
hazel and rowan which were introduced in the early and mid-
80's. Also found in these plantings are a number of willows, the
yellow and red stems of which
blaze through the winter months.
A few relic hedgerows straggle
across the rough grassland. They
are mainly hawthorn, but old
flowers like cuckoo pint may be
found beneath them.

The Westley Brook runs along the
south-eastern edge of the park before joining the Hatchford Brook
inside the airport and reappearing
as the Hatchford Brook near to
the railway line. Heron and kingfisher are said to frequent the
water courses. As well as the
brooks there are one or two areas
of wet grassland where tufted
hair-grass, rushes and reed ca-
nary-grass grow in profusion. A
less welcome feature associated
with water is the collection of
truly awful bridges which take the
footpaths back and forth across
the brooks.

A bigger bridge, in fact a red brick

46

viaduct, takes the main Birmingham to London railway line across one corner of the park. This looks better than the bridges across the streams, but even so its proportions have been spoiled by the addition of a wall above the original parapet. The Hatchford Brook trickles beneath this bridge into a short but attractive wooded valley. Unfortunately the walker needs to be concentrating on not falling into the brook at this point because the slopes beneath the railway bridge are severely eroded.

Beside the car park St. Giles churchyard has the look of a country churchyard from the outside, although the dark conifers include very few traditional yew trees. Inside it rather loses the country feel and is more typical of a town churchyard. Modern problems mean that the neatly carved wooden porch has to be secured with wrought iron gates, but at least these have been well designed to fit in with their surroundings. The church is built of sandstone and parts of it were constructed in the 14th and 15th

Cuckoo-pint

47

centuries. There may have been a wattle and daub building on this site before this. The soft sandstone is grooved in places and local legend has it that Civil War soldiers sharpened their swords and pikes here. An otherwise excellent church is - ironically - somewhat spoiled by a very unsympathetic cross set in the face of the tower. This is compensated for by a very pretty pentagonal window in the east wall.

Next to the church Old Rectory Farm provides plenty of interest. Pigs and chickens, goats and bees, and a pedigree herd of Jersey cows are all in residence. Neat beech hedges and raised vegetable beds will also be found. For 40 years from 1690 to 1730 Dr. Thomas Bray lived here. He founded the Society for the Propagation of Christian Knowledge and the charity school movement.

Sheldon Country Park is typical of urban fringe land which is being managed in a very positive way for recreation, amenity and conservation. As its new trees mature, and its streams become cleaner, it will become steadily more attractive to both casual visitors and to local people.

# Moseley Bog

MAP 139 REF. 090/821

Nine acre woodland situated three miles south of Birmingham City centre. Car park (not always open) in Yardley Wood Rd. near to its junction with Coldbath Rd. and Swanshurst Lane. Yardley Wood Rd. is off the B4217 which links the A34 and the A435. The wood is a famous Site of Special Scientific Interest. It and some of the adjacent land are also a Local Nature Reserve occupying 14 acres. Narrow, muddy paths. A fragment of Worcestershire countryside now owned by Birmingham City Council.

*Although surrounded by suburban houses Moseley Bog is self-contained enough to cast a spell over the visitor, transporting you away from the nearby hustle and bustle and back to a time - not so long ago - when this area was deep in the countryside. This is a place to stroll rather than to walk; to stretch the mind as much as the legs. In the "Endless Village" (1975) Bunny Teagle called it "a wettish peaty place" and that description holds good today. Tall trees above, woodland flowers below, water bubbling along*

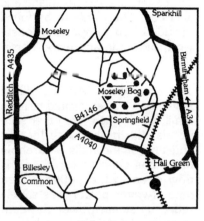

2.4 miles

*streams or lying cold beneath the leaves, and birds flitting everywhere like feathered shuttles weaving the tapestry of life.*

The heart of the site is approached from Yardley Wood Rd. across the Dell. This is an area of the Coldbath Brook valley which was filled in to create playing fields. These were never satisfactory because of water-logging. They have now been planted with young trees. Come back in a hundred years and enjoy the woodland here!

Although called "Moseley Bog" the main part of the site today is dominated by mature woodland. Oaks, birches, alders and willows tangle happily together, whilst bluebells and wood anemones carpet the ground in spring. This scene, attractive as it now is, demonstrates very well what can happen to places as towns expand. It is known that two hundred or so years ago this part of Worcestershire was heathland and acid bog. The plants to be found included bog pimpernel, lousewort, red rattle and wood horsetail.

The area where the woodland now grows was excavated to form a mill pond. There are other such ponds still in existence locally, and one of the mills - Sarehole Mill - has been restored and is now open to the public. When natural water power was superseded by steam power the dam was breached and a wet hollow was left. It is in this hollow that the woodland has developed. The scene which greets us today is therefore the result of changes

both in and around Moseley Bog over the last two centuries.

A couple of plants remain from the original bog - Sphagnum moss and wood horsetail. The latter is a delightfully graceful relative of the common horsetail which grows in abundance in the wood. In the spring its pink-tipped shoots bring an unusual complement to the bluebells. It is a plant rare in the region, and therefore it is especially welcome in this suburban site. Also still to be found is the unusual royal fern. Although recorded as growing wild here in the 18th. century the present plants are likely to be left from Victorian gardens. The remains of these gardens intrude into the eastern edge of the woodland. Presumably the frogs, which may be found in great numbers in the pool at the east-

 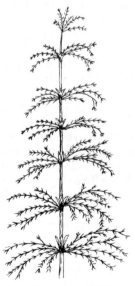

Wood Horsetail: male (left) & female (right)

50

ern corner of the wood, have also been here for centuries.

In the early 1980s this wonderful place was threatened with partial destruction by housing development. Local people formed the "Save Our Bog" campaign. This drew the attention of many others to the value of the site. Eventually common sense triumphed (but isn't it remarkable how much help common sense needs in cases like this?) and instead of the area suffering from development it became a Local Nature Reserve.

At the turn of the century things were slightly different. Being a very wet place developers went round it. They had plenty of other land available to them and speed and cheapness were of the essence. They did build houses in Wake Green Rd. It was to one of these that a family named Tolkien came to live. Their young son "J.R.R.", to be the author of the "Lord of the Rings", was five at the time. They only stayed for four years, but they were important years for the growing boy and his prodigious imagination. The countryside all around was his fiefdom, and who knows how much of it, including what is now Mosely Bog, was transposed to the vivid landscapes of Middle Earth? Any number of passages from Tolkien's books could be related to Moseley Bog today, this for instance from "The Two Towers".

*When Spring unfolds the beechen leaf, and sap is in the bough;*
*When light is on the wild-wood stream, and wind is on the brow;*
*When stride is long, and breath is deep, and keen the mountain air,*
*Come back to me! Come back to me, and say my land is fair!*

*When summer lies upon the world, and in a noon of gold*
*Beneath the roof of sleeping leaves the dreams of trees unfold;*
*When woodland halls are green and cool, and wind is in the West,*
*Come back to me! Come back to me, and say my land is best!*

Many creatures shared these woods with Tolkien as they do with us today. Bats and foxes, thrushes, warblers, woodpeckers and wood pigeons still abound. Not so likely to have been seen by him would be grey squirrels and collared doves but you may well glimpse both of these newcomers to Britain. Another animal, whose activities are very prominent, only arrived on these shores in the 1960s. This is a tiny parasitic wasp which develops inside acorns. As it does so it causes the acorn to swell and produce masses of sticky green tissue, turning brown and hard in September. In some years it may be difficult to find any unaffected acorns.

Buried deep in suburbia Moseley Bog may be said to have gone from Middle Earth to the Middle Classes. Even so there is much to be enjoyed, many things to be discovered. Its secrets lie half-hidden, waiting for you to find them.

# Kingsbury Water Park

**MAP 139 REF. 204/959**

**Visitor Centre well signed from A4097 between Junction 9 M42 and Kingsbury. Car park charge.**

*Over 600 acres of easy walking amongst lakes and woodlands. The landscape is the latest imposed by man upon the innocent Tame Valley as it wends its way to the Trent.*

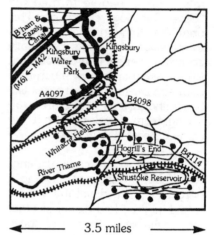

◄──────  3.5 miles  ──────►

This part of north Warwickshire forms one edge of the great plain of north east Europe. Perhaps Shakespeare knew it when he set Scene II of Act V of "Richard III" on 'A Plain near Tamworth', being as Richmond says within one day's march of Leicester. The landscape rolls gently into the distance with buildings - churches, farms, power stations, settlements - as the points of reference. Here there is space on the ground and openness in the sky. The 30 or more pools which are the main feature of this county council run country park are the legacy of sand and gravel extraction in the flood plain of the river. As buildings in the expanding Midlands towns went up so the land around the Tame went down. The mineral companies have moved on (a train journey from Birmingham to the east midlands illustrates the extent of their present operations)

and their old workings have become a rich haven for wildlife.

This is perhaps the fourth major landscape change here since the ice age. When the ice retreated the bare land was soon (in geological time) colonised by trees. No doubt beavers and otters established themselves along and in the river. After a few thousand years early settlers cleared the wildwood and flower-filled meadows and marshes for their grazing fields and crops. Mere centuries later the pastoral landscape went - ravaged by the drag lines and buckets of the mineral companies. Now after only a few decades of sand and gravel extraction the holes and hollows have been given back to nature. How long this phase will last is anybody's guess, but for now we can enjoy the young landscape as the wood-

52

lands and pools mature.

From any of the car parks easy routes take the you into the meadows, the shady woods, or along the shores of pools large and small. The heady scent of meadowsweet hangs in the midsummer air and tangles of yellow flag, water dock and Himalayan balsam line the water's edge. The latter plant shows clearly man's influence as it flourishes thousands of miles from its natural habitat. Brought to England by plant collectors in previous centuries it has become quite at home along our waterways. Too much at home for some people's liking, but children never tire of popping its "policeman's helmet" seed cases open. This activity contributes in no small measure to its ability to colonise large areas very quickly.

Near to Far Leys there are good views across the meadows to the stubby tower of Kingsbury Church, brooding over the old farm buildings below it. The church is dedicated to St. Peter and St. Paul. It has a pleasant old churchyard with some fine trees, but access to the church itself is difficult as its incongruous modern porch door is usually locked. Kingsbury's name is given because it was here that the ancient kings of Mercia were buried. Their main seat was just a few miles away at Tamworth.

Walking between the flowers of guelder rose, hedgerow cranesbill, wild rose, and elder, with here and there on the edges of the scrub and woodland areas the purple-spotted stems of hemlock, you may hear the old willows creaking their messages to the wind, or catch a glimpse of the elegant flight of common terns wheeling over the water. The terns can easily be identified if you keep in mind their other name of "sea-swallows". Although much larger than swallows they do have forked tails and a similar way of flying. At Kingsbury the species you are most likely to see is the common tern which has red legs and a black cap.

It is not only the large pools which are attractive. Some of the hidden corners hold exquisite watery gems. Near to the Broomeycroft entrance for instance a tiny pool lies close to the road. It is full of fringed water lily and has lady's mantle and cowslips in the grass around it. On a warm summer's day the brilliant colours of dragonflies and damselflies should also add their lustre to this area.

Sidestepping the rabbits, which pop up everywhere, a stroll to Mill Pool in the eastern part of the park should be rewarded with the magnificent sight of as many as twenty great-crested grebes. Their elegance and colour perhaps reflects and perpetuates the glory of the nearby court of the kings of Mercia. Their courtship rituals, with head bobbing and presentation of nesting materials, also mimics the reception of ambassadors and plenipotentiaries.

For the walker seeking solitude Kingsbury Water Park may not be

53

the place to be during a summer weekend. At other times though it is possible to escape from the crowd. On the other hand the network of good flat paths makes this an ideal place for the less agile to enjoy a close look at a good cross-section of wildlife.

# Whitacre Heath and Hogrill's End

MAP 139 REF. 215/956

**Car park inside Kingsbury Water Park close to the A4097, but access via the main entrance of the Park. Alternatively there is good parking close to the Plough Inn in Shustoke.**

*A walk taking in part of the Centenary Way. Care must be taken when crossing railway lines. Good wide paths in some parts, but narrow, nettle-fringed paths in others, not recommended for small children or wearers of shorts - at least in the summer months.*

Lakes in the Tame Valley; the villages of Hogrill's End, Whitacre Heath, Shustoke, and Furnace End; lowland farms and hedges; all combine in a kaleidoscope of typical land-use in this part of the county. Walking in this area takes in quiet countryside, contemplative views, and intimate corners. It is about eight miles from Kingsbury to Furnace End.

The path from the car park is waymarked with the bear and ragged staff logo of the Centenary Way. You leave Kingsbury Water Park to pass beneath the dual car-riageway and walk alongside the Tame. The large pools here are Coton Lakes. They are settling pools which help to clean the river by slowing down its flow. The slowing down causes contaminated silt to fall to the bottom of the pools so that the water flowing out is cleaner than that flowing in.

It is just possible that you may see a chestnut coloured duck with a brilliant blue bill here. This is the ruddy duck which, although native to north America, now breeds in various places in the midlands. Their presence is not the result of a spectacular migration but follows the escape of some birds from the Wildfowl and Wetlands Trust at Slimbridge. Ruddy duck are also called "stiff tail" ducks because of their short vertical tails. They are fast swimmers and when paddling at full speed they lower these tails, presumably for streamlining. Plenty of other birds abound. High above larks exult, whilst in the low shrubs whitethroats answer with their more scratchy song. Fighter squadrons of swifts swoop and dive around your head and jumbo-jet like herons lumber from the ground, bellies full of fish no doubt.

There is one point on the path where the view to the north east is remarkable for the complete absence of buildings. Trees and fields are all that can be seen stretching away to a low ridge. This is in complete contrast to most of the rest of the route which is dominated by the towers of Hams Hall Power Station.

The path down to Whitacre heath passes by Lea Marston purification plant. Alongside the way the water authority have planted the spectacular crimson clover. This enlivens an otherwise pretty barren stretch of the walk. Being a combined bridle and foot path, never an entirely satisfactory arrangement, it is uneven in the dry and a quagmire in the wet. Some of the life support systems of the west midlands are here - a power station, water purification works, a railway. Even so the landscape is studded with the red bricks and dark rooves of cottages and farms half hidden amongst the gentle undulations, trees and hedges.

The Swan Inn at Whitacre Heath provides welcome refreshment amidst horse brasses, old beams, false beams, and, more unusually, an anvil in one corner of the lounge.

The path now winds alongside the railway track, over a lane, and across fields to the little river Bourne. This is old farming country which has escaped the worst ravages of intensive agriculture. The hedgerows here are packed not only with the expected

hawthorn, but with blackthorn, elder, elm and field maple. No sooner do you begin to enjoy this rural scene than Nether Whitacre Pumping Station appears. This Victorian edifice once contained steam engines made by James Watt. These are now in Birmingham Science Museum.

The approach to Shustoke finds the path laid in tarmac across the middle of a large field. This curious characteristic presumably marks an old field boundary, or indicates that there were once buildings of some sort for which hard standing access was needed. To the left here is the dam of Shustoke reservoir whilst to the right is the elegant spire of Coleshill Church. In Shustoke look for the turn into Bixhill Lane almost opposite the Plough Inn. This takes you past a charming gold-fingered clock over the loft door of an old barn, through tall hedges of hawthorn, ash, and field maple with white bryony scrambling amongst them, to the reservoirs. In mid-summer the banks of the smaller reservoir are bright with flowers - pignut, daisies, buttercups, speedwell, and mouse-ear.

It is a short walk from the end of the reservoir to Furnace End. Alternatively you can can loop around the water and take the path beside the River Bourne again. Just here the river looks more like a canal, its natural origins indicated only by the alders which line the banks. Passing along by the railway, the gentle slope of the Bourne valley barely perceptible in the fields across the tracks, look out for the stile and steps at the crossing point. The footpath is ill-defined across the fields, but there is a stile to find by the road in the far left corner.

Walking through the neat hamlet of Hoggrills End brings you back to the stile by the railway bridge. Turning left will put you on the Centenary Way to Shustoke, turning right will take you to Whitacre Heath and Kingsbury Water Park.

# Hartshill Hayes Country Park ⊕

**MAP 140 REF. 317/945**

**Country park two-and-a-half miles south of Atherstone. The entrance is in the lane linking Hartshill and Oldbury in the angle formed by the B4111 to the north and the B4114 to the south. Car park (small charge). toilets, and visitor centre, on the road ("Oldbury Rd.") from Hartshill to Oldbury.**

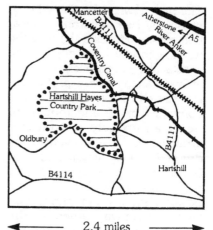

← 2.4 miles →

*136 acres of woodland and open hilltop managed by the County Council. There are woodland walks, panoramic views across Leicestershire to the Charnwood Forest, picnic places, toilets and a visitor centre.*

The car park is softened by roses, foxgloves, and brambles. The spiked metal railings around the reservoir are a little hostile, but in time the trees planted in front of them will mask their harshness. A short walk (only 30 yards or so) through shady woodland takes you from the car park on to open grassland. Sitting on one of the seats here, with Nuneaton's water supply safely tucked up in its

reservoir behind you, you can enjoy a spectacular, and somewhat unexpected view.

The ridge which you are on overlooks the Anker Valley. The next ridge forms the edge of the Charnwood Forest, with Beacon Hill to the north east. On a clear day it is said that the hills of the Derbyshire Peak District can be seen. On the flat land between the two ridges Watling St. (the A5) the Coventry Canal, and a main railway line, cross from north to south. The traffic on the A5 looks rather like the never ending line of ducks people shoot at at fairs. The canal has to be searched for, but it can be found running in front of a large white farmhouse with a grey roof. This farm house has spawned a variety of outbuildings, including modern barns and nissen hut type buildings. Closer to hand the 3M's water tower rises up behind Atherstone and a bare tree broods over the hedge at the foot of the slope.

Well marked paths lead the visitor either across the ridge to St. Lawrence's Wood, or down the slope into The Hayes. The latter has wider, smoother paths. Some of the paths in St. Lawrence's Wood are steep and slippery. On a warm summer day little clouds of small heath butterflies may rise at your feet as you cross the slopes. The bramble and willowherb flowers attract a wonderful variety of insects, including the brilliantly coloured black and yellow wasp beetle.

History and natural history mingle in and around the woods. The old coppice stools of small-leaved lime are reminders of the local trade of hat making. The Atherstone hatters used the wood from these trees to make blocks on which to mould their felt. The woodlands may have been part of the great Forest of Arden so familiar to Shakespeare. Going further back in time the name St. Lawrence's Wood commemorates the 10th. century chapel or shrine dedicated to that third century martyr which once stood close by. During the third century the Romans built kilns in the locality. That was after they had defeated

Queen Boadicea, whose last stand is reputed to have been in the valley below the ridge near to Mancetter. Even longer ago Iron Age folk constructed a hill fort close to St. Lawrence's Wood. Your footsteps are just the latest in a long line of footsteps made by soldiers, priests, lovers, and woodsmen. Like you some would pause to take in the view, reflect upon their lot, and move on.

Unlike the small-leaved limes which are indicative of ancient woodlands, and may have grown here for many centuries, most of the trees in the woods have been planted in the last two hundred years. There are plenty of lodgepole pines in St. Lawrence's Wood, and part of the Hayes is now a larch plantation. In the wetter parts of the woods alder grows and in many places hazel, elder, and holly thrive. Where the path crosses the stream in the Hayes a dead - almost "petrified" - old coppice stool lies in the stream. This is probably all that remains of an ancient alder. A feature of the Hayes is the "Clump of Oaks" - this is a group of about three dozen oaks planted around 120 years ago. The bright green leaves of the grass-like woodrush may be found beneath these. This group of plants have long white hairs fringing their leaves, and rush-like flowers.

As far as animals and birds are concerned grey squirrels abound, and you may count yourself lucky or unlucky if you spot an adder. The visitor centre has a sloughed skin of one of these beautiful creatures. They are our only venomous snake. The woods are home to many birds: coal tit, chiffchaff, chaffinch, spotted flycatcher, sparrowhawk, woodcock, jay, and wren are just a selection of what is on offer.

When you have drunk your fill of the country park an added attraction of the area is the nearby Moorwood Rare Breed Leisure Farm. This has 30 of the rarest and traditional breeds of farm animals. It is open daily from 10 a.m. to 6 p.m.

Hartshill Hayes has more wildlife, landscape, and history packed into its 136 acres than many much larger areas. It is a place where you can wander at will or merely sit and take in the view; a place to reflect upon the past or to look at today's world set out before you.

# The Weddington Area

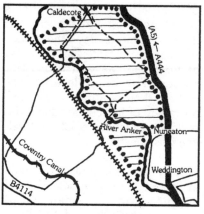

1.8 miles

**MAP 140 REF. 360/930**

**Car park at Sandon Park near to the pavilion. This is at the end of Shawe Avenue off the minor road linking the A47 and the A5 between Nuneaton and Higham on the Hill, about one mile north of Nuneaton town centre.**

*Easy walking through the fields of the Anker Valley between Nuneaton, Watling Street (the A5) and Hartshill Hayes Country Park.*

This area is the subject of one of Nuneaton and Bedworth District Council's "Your Green Track" series of leaflets. Paths are well marked. They use public footpaths, old railway lines (disused of course!) bridleways and open spaces. This is urban fringe grading imperceptibly into countryside proper.

Nuneaton's most prominent landmark is the grassed-over spoil mound from an old quarry. In honour of this prominence it has been christened "Mount Jud", the name deriving from the quarry, which was Judkins Quarry. It looms like a miniature volcano over the playing fields and the little bridge which crosses the river. On the far side of the bridge cattle may be grazing in the old water meadows. These are un-

*So typical of the Black Country's remarkably beautiful countryside—a picnicking family looks out from the seclusion of the Wrens Nest (page 12), Britain's first geological nature reserve, towards Wolverhampton.*

*Crackley Wood (page 67) near Kenilworth is unusual because it is not dominated by the usual oak or beech but contains sweet chestnut and full-sized, mature rowan and silver birch in quantity. A lovely wood.*

*There is probably no more delightful oasis of rural serenity within the hurly-burly of an often grim urban landscape than Sandwell Valley (page 34) between West Bromwich and Birmingham. This is one of the 'secret' pools.*

*In the extreme south of Warwickshire: the view north from near Brailes (page 101) towards the Cotswold village of Whatcote over ripe wheatfields.*

*Stubble and waste-straw burning after harvesting will soon be banned and a part of history. The view north-west towards Stratford-upon-Avon from Edge Hill (page 94).*

*This abandoned railway line runs between Crackley Wood (page 67) and Kenilworth Common, which since it is no longer grazed has become a perfect example of a heavily wooded common. Mostly oak over hilly countryside it offers excellent walking and picnicking.*

*Doulton's Clay Pit in Saltwell Woods Country Park (Page 18) lies just south of Dudley and offers dramatic, even startling, scenery. These old quarry workings are now being softened by nature.*

*A tiny, brilliant, overlooked jewel—Stonebridge Meadow (page 65), almost lost under curving urban highways. There are kingfishers here. It is not easy to find so be patient with your maps.*

*An angler at peace with himself and his pole (not rod, there is a distinct difference for a pole has no reel) at Rough Wood (page 32) near Walsall, and totally unaware of the M5 motorway just beyond the canal.*

*Stratford-upon-Avon is invariably crammed with tourists. Follow our recommended route and you can take your ease by this weir on the River Avon (page 81), far, far from reeking, growling traffic.*

*'Leafy Warwickshire' they say about the county, and rightly so. This is the misty-morning view south across the tree-tops from Yarningale Common (page 71).*

*Evening at Burton Dassett Country Park, (page 93) a high, wild and handsome area to wander on the edge of the Coltswold plateau beside the A41 and M40 a few miles north of Banbury.*

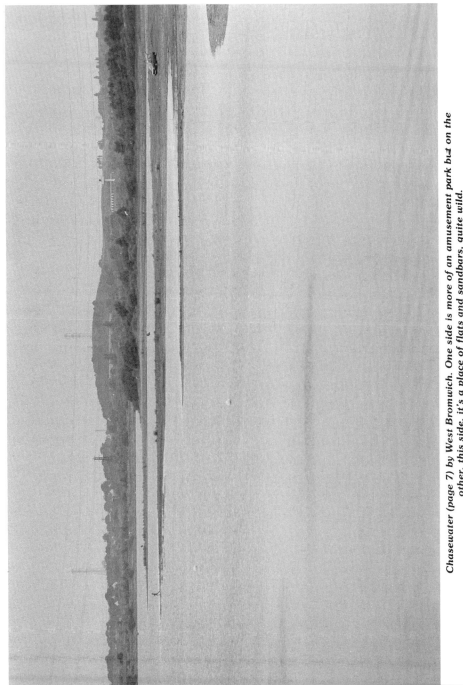

*Chasewater (page 7) by West Bromwich. One side is more of an amusement park but on the other, this side, it's a place of flats and sandbars, quite wild.*

*There are herds of cows in Sutton Park (page 39), all very docile. The place is simply gigantic, quite large enough to convince you that there's no town within a score of miles.*

*Preparing for a morning's ride at Woodgate Valley Country Park (page 23). This is only a few minutes walk from Illey and Lapal (page 21).*

*North of Walsall, almost hidden by smart suburbs, is Park Lime Pits (page 26).*
*A network of paths surround the main lake, which is popular with local anglers.*
*It's quiet and very beautiful.*

likely to be flooded now as the river has been severely engineered and lowered. This draconian treatment has divested it of natural vegetation and left it more like an imitation of a canal than the meandering country river it once was. Even so an alder and willow or two still grow close to the water, and water voles still make their homes in the steep banks.

Weddington is mentioned in the Domesday Book where it is called Watitune, thought to be a name linking it to nearby Watling St. It once had a large house called Weddington Castle which was built in the 16th. century. Sandon Park formed part of its grounds. Today the church of St. James is all that remains of the old village. For 800 years its stone font has been the scene of local christenings. The main body of the church is built in red brick and looks much more modern than its 260 years. Unusually the church tower has a chimney protruding from one of its four pitched rooves.

Alternative car parking may be had by the church (in fact a sign says "Church car park - when full use Church Hall" but I doubt this is intended to be taken literally).

Under a yew in the churchyard is buried one George William Sandon who was the Rector here for 38 years in Victorian times. Curiously he was born in Bengal and so must have returned to the family home to take up his ecclesiastical duties. The path goes past a riding school owned by another Sandon, and the park is called Sandon Park, so the family seems to have some local importance.

The fields are bounded by hedges of varying antiquity. One stretch has all the hallmarks of an ancient hedgerow whilst another looks as if it has been planted within the last 10 years. Unfortunately a lot of the hedges are flailed rather than laid. This is no doubt cost effective, and better than doing nothing, but it does leave a very unkempt appearance. In the middle of one hedgerow between two fields is a lonely Mahonia. It flowers in late winter 6000 miles from its home on the west coast of North America. If it should thrive then perhaps in two or three centuries this species will be as common around here as holly or hazel. Its success will probably depend upon whether rabbits like to eat it or not.

There is not a lot of woodland in this area but there is a small group of trees close to a bend in the river. Its mixture of Scots pine, oak and horse chestnut indicates that this is probably a small plantation. Just past these trees some old, broken and twisted cherries drip white petals on to the path in early March.

The path up to Caldecote passes a cottage with a delightful country garden whose attractions include some very noisy geese. Right opposite there is a truly massive old oak which must be several centuries old. Its huge bole supports a declining crown of heavy boughs.

A short walk across the fields brings you to the embankment of what was once the railway to Ashby-de-la-Zouch. It now has wild flowers and trees growing where once cinders and steam held sway. The old track returns you to the meadows alongside the River Anker.

# The Fillongley Area

**MAP 140 REF. 280/874**

**Car park is adjacent to the "Happy Shopper" food store on the B4098 a few yards north of the crossroads with the B4102 in Fillongley.**

*Walking on field paths and lanes through the country-side of north Warwickshire.*

Several paths lead into the sur-rounding fields from the village. Some of them are highlighted in a leaflet produced by North War-wickshire District Council in their series "Walks in North Warwick-shire". The footpaths are well marked with yellow or white ar-rows. There are plenty of stiles to negotiate. This is mixed farming country, with crops in neat fields as well as rough pastures grazed by sheep and cattle. Places which time seems to have left untouched contrast with others which bear the hallmarks of modern life.

Almost opposite the car park, by a bus stop, a stile offers a route into the fields to the west of Fil-longley. Whilst you walk above, moles shelter below, as evidenced by the numerous mole hills here. The robins singing in the hedgerow will have fed well on the worms and insects thrown up

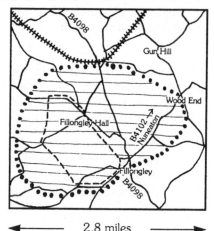

← 2.8 miles →

by the "little gentlemen in black velvet". A second stile is soon reached, its existence rendered superfluous as the hedge it is set in has many gaps.

There is more reason for the dou-ble stile which follows as it is set in a solid hedge. The dog's mer-cury at the base of the double hedgerow, the fact that it is a double hedge, and the bank upon which it stands, all point to the likelihood of it being an ancient hedgerow. In Pump Lane too - sunken as it is between high banks - there is more evidence that here are paths and ways trodden for many centuries. In amongst the tangles of holly and ivy huge elm stumps provide bat-talions of beetles and other in-

60

sects with their daily rations.

Climbing up the lane towards Manor House Farm Fillongley Hall can be seen on the opposite side of the valley. George Eliot stayed in a cottage on this estate called Bede Cottage. It may or may not have influenced her to call one of her heroes Adam Bede. In the book of that name she says that "imagination is a licensed trespasser" so perhaps we can use that licence to see her walking these paths whilst turning over in her mind the next twist of the plot.

She called Bede's home county "Loamshire" and indeed the soil here is a rich red loam. Perhaps she had the view to the Hall in mind when writing "Then came the valley, where the woods grew thicker, as if they had rolled down and hurried together from the patches left smooth on the slope, that they might take the better care of the tall mansion which lifted its parapets and sent its faint blue summer smoke among them."

Turning right by the farm takes you along a ridge where an abandoned house is slowly disintegrating. Ivy clings forlornly to its walls, and in late winter snowdrops still bloom in what was its garden. The path dips down to a small stream which is not shown on the Ordnance Survey map. It is mentioned by the name of Didgley Brook in the District Council's leaflet. A graceful alder guards the crossing and a verita-ble quiverful of arrows point the way forward.

Another discrepancy between the District Council and the Ordnance Survey is apparent at the next farm - one calls it Stonehouse Farm whilst the other calls it High House Farm. The former seems most appropriate as the oldest part of the building is red sandstone. The path follows a tortuous route through the farm buildings before crossing the lane.

As the path crosses the next field good views open out ahead. The extensive buildings of Daw Mill Colliery in the middle distance are a reminder that Warwickshire is very much a working county. Modern life intrudes as the jets approaching Birmingham International Airport begin their descent overhead. They end up close to another walk in this book through Sheldon Country Park.

The shortest route back to Fillongley takes you past both the lodge to the Hall and a cricket club. In spring the fields are full of lambs. They bleat urgently as you approach before running beneath their mothers to stare defiantly as you pass by. An old seed drill lies tangled in brambles by a stream, and the abandoned house looks down from the skyline as the double stile is reached again. The shop and the filling station bring reality back, just as the sunken lane and the view of the Hall allowed you to escape from it for a brief moment.

61

# Coombe Abbey Country Park

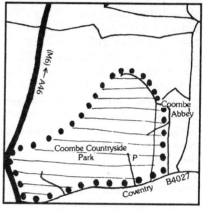

## MAP 140 REF. 404/796

**Well signposted access off the B4027 about three and a half miles from Coventry going east towards Brinklow. Car park (charge made).**

*Easy walking through historic landscape surrounding historic buildings. Woodland, lakeside and parkland routes available. Adventure playground and woodland trail. Excellent natural history interest. Toilets, refreshments, information centre and bird hide.*

1.6 miles

Coombe Abbey attracts over 300,000 visitors a year, yet it is not difficult to find peace and quiet amongst its woods and fields, or by taking a short cruise on the small boat which plys the large lake. This lake is a masterpiece of landscape design. From the terrace of the house it looks like a much larger piece of water than it really is because of the way it stretches into the distance. It is, though, long and thin, and was created by the doyen of English landscape gardeners - Lancelot "Capability" Brown. Here, as elsewhere, he took a very formal classical garden (which had been created in the 1680s) and re-imposed a naturalistic landscape.

That landscape has thrived to the point where the lake and the woodlands which surround it are now a Site of Special Scientific Interest (SSSI) which contains Warwickshire's largest heronry. Up to 20 pairs of herons regularly breed here. A very curious sight they make perched awkwardly in the lakeside trees beneath their untidy nests of twigs and small branches. Other wildlife which shares the park with the human visitors includes deer, foxes, hedgehogs, woodpeckers, kestrels and sparrowhawks.

As well as the natural landscapes which have developed in the 220 years since Capability Brown worked his magic there are formal gardens close to the house dating from the 1860's. These not only demonstrate the way in which

62

fashion goes round in circles (one century formal gardens are all the rage, the next they are wiped out, the next they are re-created) but also show the art of topiary to good effect. A pair of curious stone gateposts carved into fish welcome the visitor into one part of the gardens.

A short distance away is a splendid collection of giant redwoods from the western United States. The trees here are about 125 years old - still babies as far as redwoods go - but already they tower over almost everything else. Both Sequoia (coast redwood) and Sequoiadendron (Wellingtonia) are here. The former are believed

A Wellingtonia,
one of Britain's tallest trees

to be the tallest species of tree in the world. Both species have very soft and spongy bark. This provides sheltered roosting places for small birds, especially treecreepers, and ideal conditions for the spider Amaurobius fenestralis. This lives in holes and crevices in the bark and spins a number of bluish threads of silk which radiate from its hiding place to trap unwary insects.

Coombe Abbey itself was a Cistercian house founded in 1150. Indeed if the text in the information centre is to be believed it was founded on the 10th. July 1150. After the Dissolution in 1539 a house was built incorporating parts of the Abbey. Since then alterations, demolitions and new buildings have been commissioned. For exactly 300 years from 1622 to 1922 the owners were the Craven family. Just before they arrived in the early 1600s the young Princess Elizabeth lived here. She was implicated in the gunpowder plot but survived to marry Frederick, Elector of the Palatinate, and become the "Winter Queen of Bohemia".

When leaving the house to return to the car park just glance up at the corner of the cloister-like building by the moat where a sundial sits wrapped around the corner of two walls. As you leave the estate you may be gratified to notice that the avenue of limes along the main drive is underplanted with its replacement - if only more of these grand avenues were conserved in this way.

# Stonebridge Meadow  |⊕

## MAP 140 REF. 349/756

Parking only possible in a layby on the eastbound carriageway of the A45 (Stonebridge Highway) about 2 miles south of Coventry City centre. The layby is between the junctions with the A46 Coventry to Kenilworth road and the A423 Coventry to Banbury road.

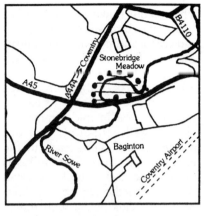

◄──────── 1.8 miles ────────►

*This is a fragile fragment of flowery meadow squeezed between a Jaguar Cars factory and the busy dual carriageway of the A45. The area is rich in insects and flowers - so much so that in 1987 it was declared a local nature reserve. As well as the meadows there is marsh, scrub and woodland, and the river Sowe. A leaflet has been produced by the City of Coventry and the Warwickshire Nature Conservation Trust.*

A stile alongside a five-bar gate takes you into the peace and quiet of the grazed meadows. The traffic's roar becomes a muted hum, instead of speeding cars there are gently fluttering butterflies, and colourful flowers replace the tarmac. Amongst the latter are lady's bedstraw and bird's-foot-trefoil. A few horses will be seen, heads down, intent on eating the

herbage rather than identifying it. They are excellent reserve managers however, keeping the sward in the right condition for many plants to thrive. Without them the grass would soon be dominated by tall coarse plants such as thistles and nettles. An added bonus is that their manure also supports a variety of dung beetles. These in turn provide a sort of meals on wings service for the local bats.

A short climb to the left takes you up a small rise rather grandly named Pikecliff Hill. The river lies below with a small wood to the left. Beyond the Jaguar plant (which badly needs screening by a belt of trees) Coventry's skyline can be seen, the old cathedral spire standing proud amongst the square blocks of the rebuilt city. The spire is virtually all that is left of the mediaeval cathedral which

65

was once a powerful ecclesiastical centre. The abbotts and bishops of Coventry rivalled those of Lichfield and Chester in their influence and wealth.

The yellow flowers of the lady's bedstraw, bird's-foot-trefoil and ragwort contrast with the purple and red flowers of rosebay willowherb, foxgloves, betony and knapweed. All of them are visited by the many butterflies which accompany you in mid-summer. A short walk through mature hawthorn and birch leads to the banks of the River Sowe. This is narrow and dark, a typically urban river - even though here it flows between fields heavy with meadowsweet and marsh thistles. It hurries on its way to Stoneleigh and its confluence with the Avon, which is about a mile and a half to the south, on the other side of Coventry's small airport. The two rivers almost surround the National Agricultural Centre in the grounds of Stoneleigh Abbey. A large clump of true bulrushes make a watery chicane for the mallards surfing along in the current. It is a little surprising to find the large flat leaves of water lily in one of the backwaters.

Although the Sowe has been lowered the old marsh lands close by retain their characteristic flowers. Yellow flag, forget-me-not, teasels, lesser spearwort and stichwort mix happily together amongst the rushes and grasses. Bright turquoise damselflies thread their way in and out of the flower and grass heads like luminous needles, orange soldier beetles cling resolutely to grass stems, and bumble bees lumber in and out of flowers, taking nectar and leaving pollen as they do so.

Further to the west there is a small woodland. This is dominated by alder trees, with a lot of nettles beneath them. Alders are typical of damp meadows and watersides in England and may be considered as one of our most beautiful trees. They have an attractive pink hue in the winter, and bear both cones and catkins. They are, in effect, nature's own Christmas trees, complete with natural baubles. The cones are not true cones, as would be found on conifers, it is just that the female flower looks like a cone. Beneath these alders nettles grow in abundance. The rich alluvial soil and the moderate shade suits them very well.

All to soon you are back at the five-bar gate and have to leave the equine reserve managers to their task. The few yards which have to be walked to the layby take you but a short distance - but they also take you from one world to another.

# Crackley Wood

**MAP 140 REF. 289/735**

**No formal car park, but plenty of space to park in lane alongside wood. This lane is off the A429 Kenilworth to Coventry Rd. near to Ladyes Hill, one-and-a - half miles north of Kenilworth town centre.**

*A fragment of ancient woodland nestling between Kenilworth and Coventry. Old trees, sunny glades, some modern plantations, and a wealth of wildflowers and colourful butterflies await the visitor. The paths are not dressed in any way, so that although they are flat and well defined they are very muddy in places.*

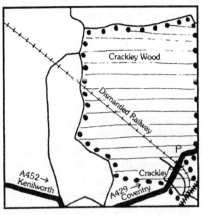

◄———— 1.4 miles ————►

The edge of the wood is marked by a hedge sitting atop a substantial bank. Beech and sweet chestnut overhang the parking area. Inside the wood ancient sweet chestnuts, heavy and gnarled, act as watchmen over the open glades. In contrast slim young birches push eagerly up to the sky, impatient for their share of the sunlight which is at such a premium in the heart of the wood. They will be long gone when the tiny seedlings of the sweet chestnuts take their places as guardians of the wood. Oak, rowan, hazel, and holly also fight

for their place in the sun. Amongst this unruly scramble it is quite a surprise to come upon a regimented plantation of sycamore trees, each with its allotted space, each the same size as its neighbour. Just to the north of the wood proper is another plantation, this one of larch trees.

Moving through the wood you may be surprised to come upon a small show-jumping ring, dominated by a huge 60 second clock. A pause to take in this somewhat unwelcome intrusion may reveal the presence of flycatchers. These small brown birds make continuous sallies from a perch high in the canopy, each time collecting a beakfull of insects. Other woodland birds here include woodpeckers, jays, and wrens.

An old railway line cuts Crackley

Wood into two. A footpath now runs where the tracks used to be. Turning to the south-west along this track provides a shady walk along a shallow cutting. The pink flowers of herb robert, pink campion, and wild roses line the path. Holly blue, speckled wood, green-veined white, and hedge-brown butterflies may accompany you. A number of routes are available from this path: to the north a public footpath runs across fields to Warwick University; continuing straight on takes you to the main road (A429) at Crackley Village; following the public footpath to the south brings you to a farm track on the opposite side of the show-jumping ring to the wood.

If you take the first of these paths through the gently rolling landscape of copses, hedges, and fields, a slight detour to the east at the lane will reveal a wonderful bank of flowers opposite to Cryfield Grange Farm. Ox-eye daisies, knapweed, mallow, cat-sear, buttercups and clovers make a splendid show in mid-summer. A black and white house snuggles in amongst the farm buildings opposite. The path to the south of the old railway along the farm track provides the shortest route back to the beginning of the walk. Woodsage grows here, and if the conditions are right hedge brown and small tortoiseshell butterflies can be numerous, especially around any thistles left to flower.

# Baddesley Clinton  ⊕

**MAP 139 REF. 201/714**

**National Trust property one mile south of Chadwick End on the A41 between Solihull and Warwick. Car park and entrance reached by turning right in Baddesley Clinton village and following signs.**

*Easy walking around small estate with lake and gardens (charge for entry). Public footpaths lead to the Stratford Canal at Kingswood (described elsewhere) and to Hay Wood (alternative parking map ref. 205/709) and Wroxall Abbey. The latter route takes in a series of con-*

← 4 miles →

*trasting landscapes - the parklands of Baddeseley Clinton and Wroxall Abbey, and the Forestry Commission plantation of Hay*

68

*Wood. The latter is claimed by some to be the last remaining fragment of the ancient Forest of Arden. This is an unlikely assertion on either ecological or topographical grounds. Toilet facilities.*

Baddesley Clinton is an archaeological gem a medieval moated manor house set in open parkland. Its survival is something of a miracle as the Ferrers family who owned it for several centuries were often in financial difficulties, caused some of the time by their adherence to the Catholic faith. As well as the house there is, standing a little apart, a small country church. Currently dedicated to St. Michael it is known that in 1634 it was dedicated to St. James, but no one knows why - or when - its allegiance was changed.

A detail from the magnificently carved huge chimneypiece (mantlepiece) that dominates the Great Hall of Baddesley Clinton

The grounds of Baddesley Clinton contain many fine parkland trees, with the symmetrical growth and wide spreading branches so typical of such estates. Near to the house is a dark lake surrounded by a variety of trees and shrubs. Ash here, Scots Pine there, and a lot of Rhododendron filling the spaces below. In summer swallows swoop over the moat, on the house side of which the huge leaves of butterbur cling precariously to a narrow ledge. The formal gardens provide a colourful diversion before taking the footpath up to the church. On one side sheep graze on pasture that retains the ridges and furrows of medieval days.

The path passes through the churchyard via a small wooden gate which unusually has a wooden catch, rather than the piece of rusty ironmongery or twisted string more normally found in such situations. The churchyard is not over-tidied and is said to have a wonderful show of bluebells in the spring. It is possible that there has been a church here for more than one thousand years. The earliest parts of the present building are thought to date from no later than the 13th. century, although major restoration took place in the 1900s and in the 1960s.

Continuing along the footpath and across the lane leads the walker into Hay Wood, past the old keeper's lodge. Blue arrows rather than yellow arrows guide you through this typical Forestry Commission plantation. The se-

vere and sensible conifers have frivolous petticoats of oak, rowan, birch and holly. Essence of pine hangs heavy in the air on a still day, and the verges of the rides may be spangled with the yellow flowers of tormentil. The thin stems of marsh thistles also line the paths. Although only a small plantation (about 290 acres (120 hectares)) Hay Wood has the atmosphere of a much larger forest with views being restricted by the closely packed trees. There is a link to the public footpath from the car park mentioned above along one of the main forest roads. The public footpath emerges from the wood on the A41 at Wood Corner Farm. This is a delightful collection of black and white buildings.

Just south of the Hay Wood car park two footpaths are signposted across open fields to the east, although their route is not well defined. The northern path goes directly into the lands surrounding Wroxall Abbey. The southern path leads into a lane from which another path goes into the Abbey grounds. There is a pub in this lane with the unusual name of "The Case is Altered". The landlady here could give no information as to why the name was given, but did volunteer that there are six pubs so named in the country.

Wroxall Abbey (or at least the building which now occupies the centre of the estate) is a public school, so the visitor must be content with walking through the grounds. Large specimen trees of oak and lime are scattered in rough grassland where a herd of Jersey cows graze and gaze large-eyed at intruders. Two features in particular catch the eye here. Around the formal gardens close to the school is a high red brick wall built in a series of convex bays. Leading away from the building is a long avenue of large oak trees. As they crest a slight rise in the distance they give the impression of continuing for ever across the countryside. This is a very fine avenue indeed, although perhaps oaks do not have quite the stately deportment of limes.

# Yarningale Common
# and the Stratford Canal to Kingswood

**MAP 151 REF. 189/659 (Yarningale Common) MAP 139 REF. 187/710 (Kingswood).**

**Car parking on the common one mile north of Claverdon, or close to the canal at Kingswood three miles east of Hockley Heath on the B4439. Toilets at Kingswood.**

*Walking in deepest War-wickshire around an ancient common, across flower-filled meadows, and along the Stratford Canal. Easy but narrow paths, with some awkward spots to negotiate.*

Yarningale Common is perched on a small hillside between the Stratford Canal and the M40 motorway. Car parking is an informal affair in the centre of the common where two lanes meet. On one side a battered sign announces that the house nearby is called "The Homestead". The name belies the somewhat grand nature of this property. The earliest record of the common is in 1482 when it is mentioned in a deed referring to land stretching from Crudehale to Yarningale. In 1950 the Lord of the Manor gave the land to Claverdon Parish Council for the benefit of local people.

The ground on the common is poor acid soil deriving from Keuper marl over Arden sandstone. This contributes to the remnants of heath which share the space with grassland, scrub and woodland. A number of narrow, un-made paths lead you on to the common. These are used by horse riders and as a result are broken up and generally muddy. The viciousness of some of the brambles is compensated for by the beautiful flowers of honey-suckle which scramble amongst them in high summer, and no doubt by succulent blackberries in the autumn.

The woodland is dominated by young oak although some older coppiced oak has now been left to grow on, forming multi-stemmed trees from the old stools. Chiffchaffs may sing their interminable song but usually defy all efforts to see them, and speckled wood butterflies patrol the edges of the paths. These wily insects often disregard human intruders but are always alert for trespassers of their own kind.

Walking over the slight rise views open to Clent, Bredon and Malvern. Continuing down the other side brings you to Valley Farm in the exquisitely named Buttermilk Lane. An interesting old barn keeps company with a flat-fronted and much-altered farm house. The farm garden is sheltered by fruit trees which spill out over the track.

Just past the farm a stile to the right beckons the walker into flower filled meadows leading to an alder woodland. Here an abundance of knapweeds, clovers, selfheal, ox-eye daisies, and birdsfoot trefoil delight the eye. They also delight the butterflies. Blues, small tortoiseshells, peacocks, and small heaths dance attendance on the cornucopia spread before them. In the wetter parts of the fields and in the alder woodland the bright blue of brooklime, the creamy white of meadowsweet, and the purple heads of marsh thistle add their contribution to the landscape. If you are lucky a marsh orchid or two may be found in these damper places. In the middle of all this a curious and rather ugly bridge has been placed. It has metal railings all around and so has to be climbed

into and out of.

Almost without warning the canal towpath is reached. Turning south (left) and walking a few hundred yards brings you to an aqueduct taking the canal over a small river. By this point the towpath has crossed to the opposite side of the canal, but climbing carefully over the sluice gate a small flight of steps is revealed which lead to the lane back to the common. The houses, converted barns, waterside cottages, and old black and white cottages in this area are the stuff that picture postcards and chocolate box lids are made on.

If a longer walk is preferred then turn to the north (right) when the towpath is reached. A pleasant walk along the canal to Kingswood will reveal a wealth of waterside plants and flowers, waterfowl, bridges, locks and lock-keepers' cottages. All of the latter have a characteristic curved roof. If you are very lucky you may see one of the local grass snakes, head held out of the water as it takes a sinuous dip. These shy animals can grow to several feet long, and swim surprisingly quickly - usually away from people. The lock and bridge walls display a number of ferns and other plants, such as wall rue and skullcap, but be careful to enjoy these from the safety of the bridges, not the edges of the locks. The gaps in the bridges are there to allow the ropes of horse-drawn boats to pass through. The Fleur-de-Lys hotel at Lowsonford is very inviting but, like a desert mirage, is not accessible as it is on the opposite side of the canal to the towpath!

The canal reached Stratford in 1816 and was at its busiest in the middle of the 19th. century. Much of this stretch is leased by the National Trust. Since 1960 they have restored it with the help of volunteers. With only the ugly intrusion of the M40 barring the way Kingswood is soon reached. Here there is a junction with the Grand Union Canal with a pound large enough to qualify as a small lake.

The harmless grass snake

# Earlswood - the heart of Arden

MAP 139 REF. 110/739

Parking available in several places, but particularly convenient at the Tanworth District Council's recreation ground between the reservoirs known as Earlswood Lakes. This is off a minor road leading to The Lakes Station. Alternatively there is a small car park next to the Reservoir Inn in The Common about one mile west of Hockley Heath. This is on the B4102 which runs from Solihull to Wood End (Map Ref. 117/738).

*An area between south Birmingham and Tanworth-in-Arden which was once part of the famous Forest of Arden. This is a delightful part of Warwickshire, full of little woods and streams, with many small fields, all set off by the waters of Earlswood Lakes. The woods include Windmill Naps and Clowes Wood (both SSSIs). The paths vary in quality and can be narrow and extremely muddy, especially where they skirt the lakes. They are definitely not suitable for wheelchairs. There are a number of stiles, but most of them are easy to climb.*

◄──────  2.6 miles  ──────►

For those used to walking in the Pennines or the Lake District it may come as something of a surprise to learn that the name "Arden" comes from the British "Ardu" meaning "high land". It perhaps demonstrates the low lying nature of Warwickshire that the slight elevation of this part of the Birmingham Plateau should be so remarked upon. The landscape wrought from the ancient forest that we see today has a notable quality which is reflected in the attempts by the local authority to guide land owners to manage it sympathetically. Pockets of woodland lie amongst small fields with thick hedgerows which, mercifully, have escaped the worst ravages of intensive farming.

Although we seek out the beauty and solitude of the woods and fields today it was not always so.

74

In centuries past such places were considered dangerous, and described as wastes. Thus Touchstone's sentiments in "As You Like It" when he has this exchange with Rosalind:

*Rosalind: "Well, this is the Forest of Arden."*

*Touchstone: "Ay, now am I in Arden; the more fool I; when I was at home, I was in a better place: but travellers must be content."*
     *(Act 2, scene 4).*

Many places in this locality have the name "green" - presumably because they were originally pasture carved out of the old forest. They include Danzey Green and Terry's Green - named perhaps for their owners - as may have been the contradictory sounding Brown's Green. The most curious of all though is Pink Green!

The larger of the two lakes is home to many water birds. An old hedgerow emerges from the water a few yards out from the path, and provides perching posts for grey herons. Beneath their im-

Heron

passive gaze great-crested grebe operate a water taxi service for their young, one parent carrying the fluffy bundles on its back whilst the other dives for food to assuage the voracious passengers. There is room for several pairs of grebe to nest alongside coot, mallard and Canada Geese. Beware though - too much attention to the birds will pitch you headlong into the mud as the narrow path is heavily worn. The woodland edges of the lakes display their ancient lineage, with hazel coppice over bluebells, dog's mercury and stichwort.

The path to Clowes Wood passes through herb-rich damp meadows. In one place a young alder coppice is neatly laid out, in another lady's smock and marsh marigolds nestle in the grass. If you go up and over the railway line be careful, there are no signs or barriers, be sure to look and listen for approaching trains. Another intrusion which Shakespeare's lovers did not have to contend with now becomes apparent - the M40, the drone of its traffic competing with the warblers, wrens and thrushes in and around the woodland.

Clowes Wood, complete with ditch and bank, is a WARNACT Reserve, but there are plenty of footpaths to take you through the trees. The canopy is fairly open, allowing birch, holly and brambles to flourish below. Lower still bluebells and bilberries carpet parts of the woodland floor. One species that seems to be doing particularly well is rowan, with many

saplings sprouting from the undergrowth. You may find alder buckthorn growing in the wood. This is an ancient woodland indicator species because it was never planted. There is a car park for the wood on the lane between Fulford Heath and Earlswood (Map Ref. 101/745). Just inside the wood the effects of numerous visitors can be seen where the undergrowth has been trampled out of existence. There is plenty of oak, rowan and holly in this part of the wood. Together with the bilberry this is reminiscent of Sutton Park.

The second (and smaller) lake is not as attractive as its companion. The banks are more severe, and a sailing club clutters the water with its buoys and boats. Even so there are plenty of water birds, and the colourful sails of the dinghies will appeal to many people. Where the path runs atop an embankment the lake is on one side and a pretty wooded cutting is on the other. A stream bubbles along the bottom of the cutting, and the opposite bank is alternately clothed in mosses, ivy or lesser celandine.

It is possible to walk parallel to the railway line (on its northern side) along a short path, not shown as public footpath on the OS map, to a short road, and then to turn right past The Lakes Station and right again to a footpath across open fields to the south-west. There are no arrows or signs associated with this path, but it is clearly marked on the map. Turning right over the motorway and right again down the drive to the Portway Golf Club brings you to Windmill Naps, another ancient woodland well worth visiting.

Some parts of Windmill Naps may be primary ancient woodland. Other areas are centuries old, and others again of more recent origin. The windmill which gave it its name no longer exists, although the mound upon which it stood can be easily located near to the southern boundary. The wood has the distinctive feel of old woodlands but needs more management to retain its rich wildlife. Rhododendron is invading some areas and coppicing needs to be restarted to provide more variety in the physical structure. Even so the oak and birch trees, the streams and ditches, the spring flowers and the singing birds unite to make a walk through here very pleasant.

# Welcome Hills

**MAP 151 REF. 216/573**

Layby provided for car parking in the lane leading to Snitterfield from the A439 about one and a half miles north-east of Stratford-upon-Avon. The lane is the first turning on the left after the drive to the Welcombe Hotel. Alternatively it is possible to walk from the Riverside car park in Stratford and approach the hills along the drive at the side of the golf course.

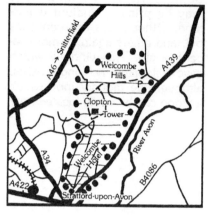

◄──────── 2.6 miles ────────►

*A delightful area, covering nearly 70 acres, through which you may wander at will. Flower filled fields, small woods and sunny glades disport themselves across the gentle slopes of the hills. Your attention may be taken by the distant views of the Cotswolds, the nearby outskirts of Stratford-Upon-Avon, or the surprising range of buildings here - from the Jacobean splendour of the Welcombe Hotel to the dignity of the obelisk or the quirkiness of Clopton Tower. The local council has done much to help you to enjoy your visit. There are good paths and gates, information boards and - if you can find a copy - a leaflet describing a*

*nature trail. This was produced in partnership with WARNACT. It offers an interpretation of the name "Welcombe" which has little to do with hospitality. It suggests that it derives from the presence of a spring or well, and the word "coombe" meaning a valley.*

From the little car park a bridle path leads towards the obelisk past Welcombe Bank Farm and Welcombe Bank Cottage. The former has a very attractive house, although it has suffered from a severe attack of windows. Roundels and bays adorn its walls in places surely not envisaged by the first builders. A curious impression is created as you walk towards it as the obelisk appears to be emerging from its roof.

78

Passing through a gate and going past an old orchard and a little white cottage brings you into the the area around the obelisk. Picnic tables, and what in the uplands would be called a mountain indicator, are to be found here. The indicator is a mine of information. From it you will learn that Burton Dassett Beacon and Edgehill are 12 miles away, Brailes I llll 12′ miles, and that the large cream building just across the main road is the National Farmers' Union insurance office!

The obelisk, which is 120ft high, is well proportioned and stands in dignified aloofness above the rough grazing pasture which surrounds it. It is obviously trying to ignore the brambles, elder and woody nightshade which cluster around its base. It commemorates members of the Philips family who owned land in the locality. They were nineteenth century politicians and businessmen, active in the north of England. Robert Philips is described as "a friend of liberty in evil days" (he lived from 1760 to 1844). One of his sons became the first member of Parliament for Manchester, another represented Bury for 22 years.

The Manchester MP was known for his interest in providing "places of recreation for the people". This would lead you to suppose that the Welcombe Hills are open to us today as a result of a generous bequest of some of the Philips land, but this is not so. The area was left to the people of Stratford by the Flowers family -

famous in this part of the Midlands for the beer originally brewed in the town. Looking at the riot of colour provided by the wild flowers in the summer this seems to be a most apposite bequest.

Moving away from the obelisk, past the rounded gables of the hotel, side stopping the scrub spilling into the pasture and climbing over a small stile you will enter Blue Cap Covert. The mixture of trees, including beech, ash and sycamore, indicate that this is more of a plantation than an ancient wood, although it has plenty of shrubs and woodland flowers within its bounds. All three species of our native woodpeckers have been recorded here. On the other side is another open field with a number of benches along its edge. Most of these are placed in such a way that the low rise in front obscures the wider views easily available a few hundred yards away.

Clopton Tower suddenly appears, looking like nothing so much as a giant chess piece - a rook with golden castellations which Lewis Carroll would have been pleased to introduce to Alice. It was once the clubhouse for the Welcombe Hills Golf Club. Passing the tower a pot-pourri of human activity presents itself. In a very short space will be found a couple of houses, an out of place stretch of Leylandii hedge, half hiding some old ivy covered stumps attempting to retain a modicum of character, a superb spreading oak tree, another information board and, finally, the surrounds of an underground reservoir.

Very soon you are back amongst the hawthorns and the wild roses, joining the bees and the butterflies in enjoying the flowers, which here include the unusual yellow spikes of agrimony. The name of this tiny member of the rose family comes from the greek "argemos" meaning cataract, as in the eye disease. Ancient herbalists used the plant as a treatment for this. Mushrooms push through the grass, chiffchaffs and robins sing from the trees and meadow ants go about their business beneath your feet.

Walking back to the car park you may reflect on whether or not Shakespeare trod the same path. The family had as many connections with Snitterfield as with Stratford, and the Welcombe Hills lie between the two. Never as important as Stratford, Snitterfield did have its own market and fair. The poet's grandfather Richard lived through four reigns there. He was a tenant of land belonging to the Ardens, and his son John (William's father) married Mary Arden. John Shakespeare was a man of some standing in Stratford but was known to have retained property in Snitterfield and nearby Ingon. It was not until he fell upon hard times in the late 16th century that he disposed of his land at Snitterfield, and then only to a nephew. Perhaps the bloody iniquities of "Titus Andronicus" - written about 1589 - were Shakespeare's reaction to his father's misfortunes.

# The River Avon near to Stratford |

MAP 151 REF. 204/533

Parking available in lay by
(RAC telephone point as
shown on the Ordnance Survey map) on B4632, just
over one mile south of Strat-
ford-on-Avon town centre off
the A34. Alternative parking
at Greenway car park Seven
Meadows Rd.alongside public
footpath utilising disused
railway line on the other side
of the River Avon (REF.
197/540). This is off the
A4390, a new dual carriageway which has no road number on the OS map.

*Generally very easy walking
through the fields bordering the River Avon. Long
stretches of footpaths without stiles or gates. The
paths are well marked with
yellow arrows and - where
appropriate - with the sym-
bol for the riverside walk
from Stratford to Marlcliff.
Stratford District Council
have produced a leaflet
describing this walk, which
is nine miles long. You will
find gently undulating
fields in open landscapes
dotted with trees and buildings, but containing
secluded corners by both
the Avon and the Stour.
Refreshments and toilets
available at the Shire Horse*

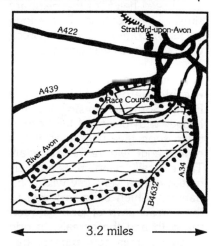

◄——— 3.2 miles ———►

*Centre and Farm Park.*

A short walk down the B4632
takes you over the River Stour by
Clifford Chambers Bridge. The
shallow waters ripple over a sandy
bed beneath the bridge whilst
above the water willows whisper
confidentially in the gentle
breezes. On the opposite side of
the road the Shire Horse Centre
is well worth visiting.

The hedgerows and verges here
are rich and diverse. There is the
welcome sight of elm doing well
despite the clinging attentions of
ivy, and spreading out from the
bottom of the hedges you may
find campions, ground ivy, mallow, Jack-by-the-hedge, dead nettles and the delicate little Geranium dove's-foot cranes-bill. The
latter plant seems to be unnecessarily burdened with supposed

81

likenesses to two birds. Why dove's-foot is a bit of a mystery, but the cranes-bill is easily explained as it is related to its scientific name of Geranium. The elongated seed heads of the plant are similar in appearance to the long beaks of cranes - and the Greek word for cranes was geranos.

A metalled farm track leads into the big fields of Milcote Hall Farm. Some promising looking hedges with plenty of tall holly in them soon give way to stretches of field edge with no hedges at all. The clinically clean crops are permitted only a very few wild companions which cling forlornly to the narrow strip of land between the path and the cereals. In one or two places cow parsley has succeeded in gaining a foothold, its white flowers looking like lines of surf along the edge of a green sea. With so many of our native trees and shrubs having disappeared from the hedgerows, insult is added to injury in the cottage gardens which have pines, sumachs, even Cypresses and Italian privet in them.

The reputation of the English landscape is saved by the neat buildings of Milcote Manor Farm, the slender spire of All Saints Church Luddington threading its way through the trees, and the Avon itself hiding shyly behind skirts of green willow. Silver water scrambles its way over a weir, swans and ducks pick their way serenely between the boats moored above the lock and herons may be seen standing motionless in the ploughed fields.

A footpath runs along the river back to Stratford through fields grazed by cows and sheep. The presence of livestock mean that stiles now have to be negotiated at each field boundary. This path is part of the way-marked route from Stratford to Marlcliff. In the summer the grazing animals are kept company by squadrons of swallows which skim the ground catching insects rising from the grass.

The river bank is lined with huge pollarded willows, whilst in the water grow true bulrushes, water mint, branched bur-reed and water lilies. Enjoyment of these natural beauties is temporarily interrupted by the ugly bridges which used to take a railway over both the Avon and the Stour close to their confluence. The bridges' saving grace is a fine show of wall rue which decorates their brickwork wherever it can gain a foothold. The old railway track is now a footpath and cycleway. It can be used to cross to the far bank to gain access to the footpath to Luddington.

The village of Luddington is a tiny collection of pretty cottages, some with beetle-browed thatch above their little windows, and some with their half-timbering painted black and white. The little church has its spire positioned in the middle of one side rather than, as is more usual, at one end. Also unusual is a wooden rather than stone memorial to one "A.H. Bullen - Gentleman and Scholar". He died on the 22nd February 1920 - Baden-

Powell's birthday, dedicated by the scout movement as "thinking day". Not for the first time in Warwickshire the churchyard reveals an avenue of truncated lime trees along the main path. The yew trees in the churchyard have all been trimmed into wine glass shapes.

On the other bank towards Stratford a fine piece of woodland hangs precariously on to a high and steep slope above the river. Oak, blackthorn and field maple grow above cow parsley and bluebells. A steep path with a flight of steps leads down through this wood to the side of a lock by another weir. This is the very edge of Stratford, with the town centre within easy reach and a variety of footpaths available to get you back to your parking place.

# Napton on the Hill | ⊕
# and the Grand Union and Oxford Canals

### MAP 151 REF. 464/612

The village of Napton on the Hill is situated just south of the A425 about three miles east of Southam. Car parking available near to the church down a single track road right off Butt Hill, which itself leads to the village from the A425.

*From Napton good walks may be had across fields to Southam and Stockton, or along the towpaths of the two canals. The walking is easy, there are some fine views over the county, and the little church of St. Lawrence close by the windmill is well worth a visit. Southam lies between this walk and the one around Ufton*

The church sits atop Napton's hill, close enough to heaven to

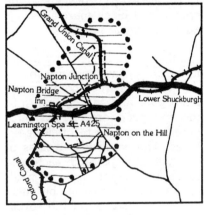

←——— 3.2 miles ———→

need only a short tower. Plenty of the original Norman building remains, in particular the north wall of the chancel (which is rubble rather than dressed stone). This wall is very thick and has tiny windows set into it. Local legend has it that the church was to be built lower down in the village but that one night the stones were moved to the hilltop by unseen forces. No doubt generations of villagers

83

toiling up the hill to Sunday services have had cause to curse those unseen forces, and to wish the original site had been used.

The Diocesan authorities make a brave effort at environmental management in the churchyard. Rules are displayed about the types of stone which may or may not be used for headstones. Marble should not be used, neither should black, red or blue granite. Grey granite is thought to be "not fitting but not forbidden". It is hoped that lime, Hornton, York or Forest of Dean stones will be used. Their strictures do not seem to be heeded - everywhere in the churchyard black marble facings adorn the gravestones!

Another losing battle being fought in the churchyard concerns the little avenue of trees between the main gate and the church. Into this tiny space someone has introduced an avenue of - of all trees - limes. The result is two lines of 12' high lime pollards, each bole forlornly sprouting from its mutilated top in a desperate but futile effort to assume its full forest grandeur.

Close to the church is Church Leyes Farm - an organic working farm which is open to the public. (Open every day except Saturday, adults £1.00, Senior citizens 75p, children 50p). Produce for sale includes eggs, timber and firewood.

A few yards away the fine windmill looks out over the farms and villages of central Warwickshire, its white sails forming a promi-

nent landmark for miles around. Napton Hill is only 525' high, but that was enough to encourage the builders of the first mill more than 500 years ago. Today we shilly and shally about wind energy - looking at cost-benefit analyses, comparing it to coal and oil power - whereas in simpler times folk just built windmills on the chance that they would work. In this case they were lucky. The mill is now a private home and is not open to the public.

It is best to retrace your steps from the windmill and take the path down the hill on the other side of the church (This is named "Hillside" but there is only a sign at the bottom.). If you do take the path down near to the windmill then you have to negotiate a small industrial estate. The latter route does, however, give you the opportunity to see a curious line of huge boulders at the foot of the hill. They look as if they have been thrown down from the top - perhaps the unseen forces which moved the stones for the church up the hill threw these down out of the way. This route also provides a sight of the smart new steel boats awaiting buyers at Peter Nicholls Steel Boats Ltd. Whichever way is chosen it is necessary to cross to the towpath of the Oxford Canal. This path can be muddy, and threatens to pitch the walker into the canal at various places where it slopes towards the water.

Refreshment may be had at the Napton Bridge Inn, where the canal widens out sufficiently for there to be a "winding hole" (a turning place for canal boats). Ridge and furrow fields come right down to the water's edge opposite. The heady scent of meadowsweet fills the air in summer, whilst in the spring moorhen busy themselves with nest making. Some of these birds may be busy finding other moorhen's nests to lay their eggs in. They are a bit like cuckoos in this respect, except that they will not lay in the nests of other species, but only other moorhens.

A short walk across open fields (beware the lack of footpath arrows here) brings you to Napton Reservoir hiding behind a low bank. Built to supply water to the canals it now also serves the pur-

pose of providing a home for birds. Reed buntings flit around the reedbeds, and waterfowl such as tufted duck, Canada goose and coot grace its water. Handsome great-crested grebe may also be seen here. In March and early April two or three pairs may be indulging in their elaborate courtship rituals.

There is barely time to enjoy the birds before reaching Calcutt Top Lock on the Grand Union Canal. Here all is hustle and bustle as boats wait their turn to pass through the lock. Crews offer each other much unsolicited advice as they manoeuvre around and between moored boats and the lock gates. You must pick your moment to cross to the op-

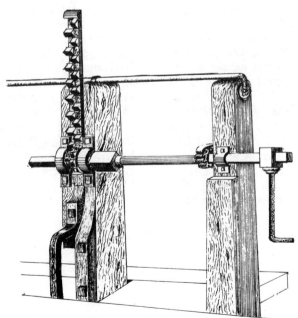

Sluice winding
mechanism at the lock gates

85

posite side of the canal using the tops of the lock gates as a foot-path. A discreet sign near to the shop points the way with the legend "Napton Nature Trail only". (A leaflet describing the Nature Trail won first prize in the Warwickshire Nature Conservation Trust's 1990 Village Nature Trails Competition).

The towpath leads to the junction of the two canals. This is the start or finish of the southern section of the Oxford Canal, depending upon which way you are travelling. For about five miles east of here the two canals are one waterway. They split again at Braunston Junction. The various waterways have existed for a long time but the name Grand Union Canal is of fairly recent origin. It came into being in 1919 after a number of other canals amalgamated. These included the Regents, Grand Junction and Warwick and Napton Canals. The Oxford canal was one of the last canals James Brindley worked on. He died whilst it was under construction in 1772. The canal reached Napton in 1774, Banbury in 1778 and Oxford in 1790. The Cruising Guide to the Oxford Canal says:

*"On 1st January 1790 the bells rang out over Oxford as the band of the County Militia headed a fleet of boats into the new City Basin and the canal officially opened. By July there existed a canal link from Manchester to Oxford... "*

The good natured banter of today's pleasure boaters must be a sharp contrast to the swearing, sweating boatmen of years gone by whose living depended upon being first into the locks. It is thought that there are more pleasure boats on the Oxford Canal today than there were working boats in its commercial heyday.

A final amusing twist to all of this activity is provided by British Waterways. A sign on the towpath leading back to Napton exhorts "All craft please read" - now a boat that can read would be a smart craft indeed.

Back in the village look for "Hillside" again. This will take you back through its kissing gates to the church. In spring laughing lambs mock your panting efforts to climb this short sharp hill, but you can take a breather to look back at Napton Reservoir below, before St. Lawrence's church comes into view at the top of the hill.

# Ufton and the Itchen Valley    $\oplus$

## MAP 151 REF. 377/615

Walking through fields and lanes between Ufton and Southam. No formal car parking but room to park safely in the lane which links the A425 in Ufton with the B4452 towards Harbury. Ufton is about three miles east of Leamington Spa on the A425.

*Easy walking through open countryside skirting a nature reserve and including rough pastures, a small wood, and a country estate. Plenty of mud and plenty of stiles and gates - some of the latter may not have been opened for years and have to be climbed. When doing so please remember to use the hinged end.*

Ufton Fields is a wetland reserve managed by WARNACT. Access is by permit only but the character of the Reserve can be enjoyed from the public footpath which runs close by. The area was a clay quarry from 1952 to 1955. Since then a wide variety of wildlife has moved in, so much so that it is now an SSSI and a Local Nature Reserve. The birds here include kingfisher, green woodpecker, ruddy duck and grasshopper warbler. Animals such as great crested newt and muntjac deer

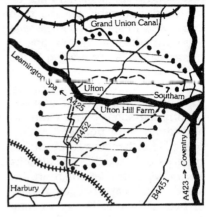

◄——— 3.6 miles ———►

are happy to make Ufton Fields their home, and you may be lucky enough to see marbled white and grizzled skipper butterflies.

Some of the fields close to the Reserve are in sharp contrast to it. They have the sterile look of intensively farmed land, with their neat rows of cabbages, and a mixture of flailed hedgerows and no hedges at all. A house called "Flax Hill" may stand as a reminder of what used to be grown around here - and may be again soon. The fields of gold oilseed rape which so dominate the English countryside in late spring are starting to give way to the gentler blue of flax. It is strange how marathon meetings and financial deals struck in Brussels and Strasbourg can so alter the face of the English countryside.

If you wander up to the "B" road the water tower by the sign for the village of Harbury will point the way to the footpath across Ufton Hill Farm. The finger post has woodworm, its letters are almost indecipherable but the path does exist. In spring your passage will be marked by the bleating of the ewes and lambs grazing in the rough pasture. In an adjoining field a profusion of rushes signify that even in this hard worked countryside some corners remain undrained, and perhaps, unimproved. Further away one of the county's old windmills sits atop its low ridge, a rare landmark in this world of fields and hedges. A hare or two is likely to be seen coursing away from your intrusion.

There is a distinct lack of yellow arrows to help you past Ufton Hill Farm, but if you keep the farm on your left (when walking north east towards Southam) the path can be picked up without too much trouble. The rooves of the farm's low barns are encrusted with golden-yellow lichens, and rooks and starlings wheel around the farmyard. Somewhat surprisingly a bright orange windsock sits in one of the fields. Perhaps someone from here takes part in those wheelings and dealings in Brussels, but has to be back to milk the cows every evening. Those same cows, together with their equine cousins, make every gateway a sea of puddled mud.

A landfill site occupying an old quarry does little to enhance the area past the farm, and has caused the footpath to be diverted

to boot. It regains its old way to take you across the west side of the Itchen Valley, through ridge and furrow to the A425 east of Ufton. Over the road lies Stoney Thorpe Hall, hiding behind a small woodland in the middle of its parkland. Fine limes keep company with old sweet chestnuts and beech pollards in the short-cropped grassland. Noisy rooks chatter away as they wheel around several small rookeries.

The most redundant stile in the world sits in a field at the end of a hedge, but with open grass on three sides! Just ahead the skyline is dominated by woodland. Its welcome coolness enfolds you together with woodland birds and flowers. Beneath tall Scots pines and oaks the peace is only broken by the gentle sounds of the birds and the distant lowing of cattle. In springtime violets, lesser celandine, primroses and bluebells add to the special magic only found in English woods.

The B4452 offers alternative parking on the verge near to the stile at the end of the footpath (MAP REF. 392/624). Over the road the path skirts the edge of Ufton Wood. With its classic bank and ditch, dog's mercury, primroses and bluebells, oaks, hazel and holly, this has all the hallmarks of an ancient wood. Plenty of paths lead into the heart of the wood. On the other side of the path the village of Ufton comes into view, the squat church tower, tall chimneys and ubiquitous Wellingtonias marking its position. A more surprising feature is the Petanque and Boules Club attached to the White Hart pub.

At the back of the church a set of old stocks lie, waiting in vain for felons and ne'er-do-wells. No doubt the local magistrates occasionally cast longing glances at these ancient deterrents, wishing that some of their modern "clients" could be subjected to a spell within their wooden embrace.

The stone-built church of St.Michael and All Angels is surrounded by a disappointingly neat churchyard, all control and no character. Just around the corner a tiny oak tree bears a plaque indicating that it was planted in 1951 - it is called the "Festival Oak". It has made remarkably little growth in the 40 plus years since it was planted, and is nowhere near outgrowing the circle of metal railings within which it is imprisoned.

A footpath leads from the village, past the nature reserve, and back through a kissing gate to the lane where your vehicle is parked.

# Lighthorne and Chesterton

## MAP 151 REF. 343/559

**No formal car parking available, but there is space in the lane leading to the public footpath out of Lighthorne (turn left just before the pub), or at the Antelope public house in the village. Alternatively cars can be left at the end of the lane which runs past Chesterton Church at 580/359. Lighthorne village is to the south of the old A41 (now the B4100) about eight miles south-east of Warwick.**

*This is typical central Warwickshire countryside. Fields and copses, old farms, gentle contours, a folly of sorts and a couple of churches will be encountered. A surprising amount*

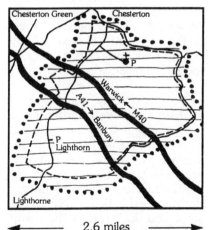

◄——— 2.6 miles ———►

*of the footpaths are on metalled paths or roads, but there are some field paths and stiles. Two aspects of human activity recur over and over again on this walk. The first is the current mania for planting*

89

*conifers, whether it be for commercial forestry, on estate roads, or in church-yards and gardens. The second is the truly amazing things people do with doors and windows in what would otherwise be reasonably attractive houses and cottages.*

Lighthorne entered from the north off the B4100 is a pleasant stone built village, close enough to the Cotswolds to be influenced by them. The footpath starts at the end of a cul-de-sac past a sign which says "private drive" at the old school house. Curiously the path is indicated by a sign prohibiting cycles from being ridden along it, rather than by a positive sign indicating a public footpath. At least there is a sign, for most of the time you will have to rely on the Ordnance Survey map as footpath indicators are a rarity.

The path quickly takes you to Lighthorne Heath between a miniature prairie on the right and what once would have been described as "waste" on the left. Fortunately we have a more enlightened view today of poorly drained rushy fields. No doubt snipe and duck rest in the damp hollows of the marsh. The path squeezes through Lighthorne Heath, modern houses just failing to impede it. Once over the main road the first piece of missing path is encountered (or I suppose to be strictly accurate is not encountered). You can either tackle the large field which has swallowed up this path or, more con-

veniently, stay on the metalled surface, go past Kingston Grange and take the bridge over the M42 to Kingston Holt.

Whoever owns and manages the land to the west of the motorway seems to care little for amenity or beauty. Once over the bridge however there is a complete contrast around Kingston Holt, even though both properties retain nissen huts from the Second World War when there was a transit camp here. A beautifully kept garden adjoins the house and the combined footpath and bridle path is clearly marked. In midwinter and spring you may see a few lambs here. The hedgerow alongside the little brook is rich with hips and haws, eagerly sought out by handsome fieldfares and redwings.

A little wooden gate signals the end of the waymarking again. You are now confronted by a vast field with not a trace of the footpath. To the left is a large stag-headed oak, probably marking where a hedge used to run. It is best to skirt the field edge to the left rather than head straight for Kingston Farm. In so doing you can easily regain the public footpath to the north-west of the farm where it runs along a narrow metalled lane to a series of fish ponds. This lane is bordered by an avenue of small poplars which, although only about 12 feet high, are already leaning at an angle which makes it doubtful that they will reach maturity. They seem to be somewhat unsuitable for this exposed position.

In winter a fiery dogwood amongst sedges and reedmace indicates the start of a series of elongated ponds associated with a large house. These ponds, and the land around them, have been planted up with a variety of ornamental shrubs, leaving only a ruff of willowherb around the shores and the islands. There seems to be a distinct shortage of waterfowl on the ponds, although a family of swans may be in evidence. The path goes on to the little church of St. Giles standing all alone on a slight rise. It is here that the alternative car parking will be found. Between the house and the church the first view is obtained of the ornamental windmill on top of windmill hill. This windmill is attributed by some to Inigo Jones, although others say that too many things in this part of the country are so attributed without sufficient evidence. Be that as it may the churchyard contains a very fine restored arch also said to be by Jones. The arch is certainly unnecessarily ornate, and is set in quite a dramatic way. As Inigo Jones was first and foremost a theatrical man then maybe he did have a hand in this.

The church is long and low, with a small tower and a roof embellished with battlements. It is almost like a shrine to the Peyto family who were obviously of some importance locally. The headstones in the churchyard are all lichens and no dates as they are mainly sandstone which does not weather too well. Over the door to the church is written the less than welcoming "See and be gone about your business".

Moving up to Chesterton Green the path runs between two farms which seem to have got themselves crossed over. On the right Lodge Farm boasts a fine flock of sheep, whilst on the left Ewefields Farm proclaims that it is the home of a prize herd of Fresian cows! The handful of houses and cottages here display that peculiarly English determination to be different, even to the extent that just one of them has a thatched roof. Once again the path takes its leave and it is best to turn to the left and follow the lane over the motorway, leaving Barn Hill with its two lonely trees on the right.

Immediately over the motorway a U-turn to the right finds the bridle path arrows which guide you around Chesterton Wood. You have one last chance to contemplate the windmill before it disappears from view. Barn Hill is now in front of you and to the left, whilst on the distant skyline Leamington Spa throws up a tall block of flats. Around the wood a ditch and bank indicate that this is more than likely to be an ancient woodland. A fringe of coppice woodland, mainly hazel, ash and oak, screen the commercial conifers within. It is possible to walk through the wood from the western edge, between conifers on the left and traditional coppice woodland with oak and ash standards on the right. Where the paths meet in the middle of the wood a tiny lodge stands with a good clump of common polypody on its roof. Nearby a patch of Rhododendron innocently sits awaiting its chance to rampage through the wood, as it surely will if not checked.

Back over the B4100 the path passes through sheltered fields with hedgerows filled with wild roses and wild privet. This is prime hunting country and the field gates are accompanied by lowered fences affording easy passage to riders. Crossing the short-cropped sheep pastures wide views open up over the county to the north-east of Stratford-upon-Avon. Suddenly you come upon the low tower of the church, and below it - all unexpected - lies Lighthorne. The

church - dedicated to St. Laurence - and churchyard are neat and tidy. In 1291 it was valued at £17.6s.8d. Its restoration in 1876 no doubt cost considerably more than this. In the churchyard the traditional yew trees are accompanied by a giant redwood. A couple more of these huge trees, already outgrowing everything else around, are planted nearby.

Here is suburbia exported to the countryside with an assortment of bungalows, cottages and houses. That part of Lighthorne close to the church lacks the charm and character of the older part. Be that as it may a short stroll soon brings you back to the Antelope and your waiting transport.

# Burton Dassett Hills Country Park | ⊕

## MAP 151 REF. 395/521

Car parking at random within the country park. The hills - which are very prominent - are just over one mile east of Temple Herdewyke, which is about eight miles south of Leamington Spa. They straddle the lane off the A41 leading from Temple Herdewyke to Farnborough. Easy access from Junction 12 of the M40 via the B4451 and the A41.

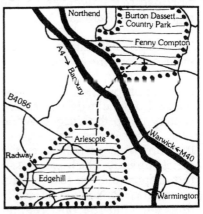

◄——— 3.4 miles ———►

*100 acres of open countryside managed as a country park by Warwickshire County Council. Although the highest of the five hills is only 200 metres high there are magnificent views over the relatively flat surrounding countryside. One of Warwickshire's finest churches - All Saints Burton Dassett - is close by. Footpaths lead away from the hills to Arlescote and Edge Hill. Refreshments, information and toilets available. Small charge for car parking.*

Some of the information relating to the country park talks of "rugged hills" and "peaks" being "battered by the elements". If this conjures up visions of a place like Kinder Scout or Skiddaw, scoured by the icy blasts of winter, then fear not. The Burton Dassett Hills are of a much more gentle disposition, almost struggling to drag themselves up from the plain around them. No doubt they can be bleak and windswept, but the sheep nibbling away at the short grass cannot have such an uncomfortable time of it as their Peak District or lakeland cousins.

On a fine day in summer those sheep may have to fight for their bit of grass. The citizens of Warwickshire disport themselves all over the hills with their children, kites, dogs and picnic gear. The policy of allowing open access for vehicles as well as people detracts from what would otherwise be a very pleasant area. In midweek, or on days when the weather mitigates against sitting in the sunshine, the hills come into their own. Open views and bracing

93

breezes reward the walker who cares to explore Pleasant, Bonfire, Windmill, Magpie and Harts Hill. Views stretch away for over 50 miles to the Clee Hills in Shropshire, as well as to the slightly closer Malverns.

The reddish soil betrays the presence of iron ore and the many hollows in the hills are the remains of old quarries. Ore was extracted from the middle of the last century up to the Second World War. There is now little sign of the narrow gauge railway or the aerial ropeway which were used to transport the ore to the main railway near to Northend. Despite the quarrying the hills remain botanically rich, the pastures never having been either enclosed or improved. That richness must be under threat from the free ranging sheep who seem intent upon imparting a billiard table-like smoothness to the grassland.

No visitor should leave without seeing All Saints Church. Known as the "Cathedral on the Hills"

this is a deceptively large Norman and medieval church which has miraculously escaped the depredations heaped upon most similar buildings. Much of the building dates from the late 12th century. An unusual feature is the rise of 15' from west to east. The whole place has an open, airy feel about it, as befits a church tucked in amongst hills. The relative openness and plainness inside, combined with the good light, reveals the architecture - a feature so often obscured in smaller, more ornately decorated, churches.

A notice in the churchyard proclaims success in the best kept churchyard competitions. Fortunately this has not resulted in over tidyness or sterility. There is a pleasantly informal atmosphere, with speedwell and daisies allowed to scramble around the local stone headstones. One of these commemorates Thomas Bishop who died in 1859 aged 100. You may search a good many churchyards without finding another centenarian.

# Edge Hill

**MAP 151 REF. 382/474**

**Small car parking space outside Ratley village hall in Chapel Lane and School Lane, just to the south east of the minor road which runs across the top of Edge Hill between the B4086 and the A422 to Banbury.**

*Plenty of walking on and around the famous Edge Hill (the site of the first major battle of the English Civil War on October 23rd 1642). Many stretches of footpath completely obscured by crops, signposting not good, and a lot of fences and gates to scramble over where there ought to be stiles. To compensate there is plenty to see and to interest the observer. Delightful hamlets, beautiful woodlands and panoramic views of the countryside, all combine with an intangible, but very real, sense of history in this quiet countryside close to the Oxfordshire border.*

Ratley is an attractive village lying almost inside the right angle of the "L" shaped Edge Hill. Neat tiles and steeply angled thatch cap its buildings. To the north-east paths lead to the top of the ridge above Arlescote. A narrow wood

clings precariously to the ridge before tumbling down the far slope. In late spring the pink campions and wild roses of the hedgerows are joined in and around the woodland by the yellow flowers of archangel and sheets of white wild garlic flowers. A glance at the hedgerows between Ratley and the wood reveal that this area was once all wooded, as many woodland species can still be found bordering the fields.

Arlescote is a tiny hamlet, consisting of a few houses scattered somewhat haphazardly around a bend in the lane leading to Avon Dassett and Fenny Compton. The

Foot soldier, or infantryman, of the Civil War 1642

95

largest house is Arlescote House - which, unusually these days, still has one of its gateways identified as a "tradesmens' entrance". The present building dates from the late 17th century. Its predecessor provided a refuge for the 12 year old Prince Charles (later Charles the Second) at the height of the Battle of Edgehill. (The OS map gives the name of the hill as "Edge Hill" (two words) but in the literature the battle is always referred to as "Edgehill").

From Arlescote it is possible to continue walking north to Burton Dassett Country Park. The way lies across a variety of fields and pastures, with the stone tower on top of the Burton Dassett Hills showing the way to go. Where the footpath crosses a small stream the banks may be bright with pink campions, white cow parsley and yellow buttercups. A massive old willow pollard stands here gently degenerating, as it does so providing a home for all sorts of plants pretending to be epiphytes. These include dandelions, white dead-nettles, wild roses and blackthorn.

If you time your walk for about the middle of May a curious optical illusion may be experienced. Where the M40 motorway is crossed there are fields of oilseed rape. The motorway lies in a cutting between two such fields. As it is approached the bright yellow fields look like a seamless cloth of gold, with nothing as vulgar as a motorway anywhere within sight. A less welcome result of this agricultural activity is the disappear-

ance of the footpath immediately over the motorway bridge. It is best to divert to the left, past another surprise - a small pool complete with fishing platforms and resident mallards.

Considering its importance in our history there is remarkably little evidence of the Battle of Edge Hill anywhere in the area. For those who wish to relate the present day landscape to the events of October 1642 then a visit to the Edgehill Battle Museum - a few miles away at Farnborough Hall, Farnborough, near Banbury - is advised before starting to explore. (The museum is open on Wednesday and Saturday afternoons from April to September). It sells a "Guidebook to the Battlefield" which costs £1.00.

To reach the site of the battle leave Ratley along the lane to the north west, then turn left along the top of the ridge. A mock castle - which is now a public house - stands at about the point where King Charles raised his standard before the fighting started. Moving down the steep escarpment the village of Radway lies half hidden in trees slightly to the right. Radway Grange was substantially as it is today on the day of the battle. Looking beyond the village a flat plain - once known as the Vale of the Red Horse - stretches away to a distant view of Warwick.

A peaceful walk down this slope in evening sunlight, through buttercups and daisies, accompanied by birdsong, must be a far cry from the day when 30,000 ill-trained troops engaged in what was to be the first of more than 600 armoured clashes in the nine years of our civil war. Evidence that we have learned little since then occupies the flat plain ahead. It is ironic that the area where most of the fighting took place is now occupied by a huge ammunition depot - CAD Kington. The neat rows of bunkers seem to stretch for miles, in the same way perhaps that the Parliamentary forces did in the eyes of the cavaliers.

That dynamic fensman Oliver Cromwell was still learning his military trade here. He was a captain of horse in the Earl of Essex's army. This would have given him command of about 70 men - but in any case he did not arrive until late in the day.

Radway has a collection of cot-tages, some thatched, clustered close to a village green complete with a duck pond. Its church, dedicated to St Peter, was built in 1866, the earlier church having been demolished. Even so it has a number of yew trees overhanging the path to the door. Inside the church is the famous Kingsmill Monument, erected in memory of one of the casualties of the battle - Henry Kingsmill. The inscription reads: "I have fought a good fight, I have finished my course, henceforth is laid up for me a crown of righteousness."

For those of you who find so much to occupy your time in this fascinating corner of Warwickshire that you neglect other matters, you may care to recall the prayer of Sir Jacob Astley before the battle - "O Lord! Thou knowest how busy I must be this day. If I forget Thee, do not Thou forget me."

# Honington and Idlicote

## MAP 151 REF. 267/423

No formal car park but there is plenty of parking space on the wide verge of the lane leading south from Honington to Fell Mill Farm and on to Willington. Honington is just to the east of the A34 between Treddington and Shipston-on-Stour. The footpaths provide fairly easy walking, with long stretches free of stiles or gates, although they are muddy in places. You are recommended to carry a map as there is a distinct lack of signposts, and in one or two places a distinct lack of footpath.

*Beautiful countryside langorously stretching itself over gentle hills. Farms, small villages and little woodlands close to the River Stour play host to singing birds and gently fluttering butterflies in this quiet corner of south Warwickshire. The ancient hamlet of Idlicote lies atop its small rise as if the 20th. Century had never happened.*

What business a farm has to call itself "Fell Mill Farm" in deepest Warwickshire no one knows, but there it is, hard by the River

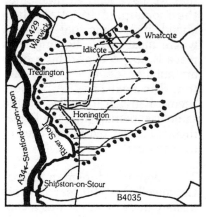

← 3.6 miles →

Stour. The waters of the river tumble over a little weir close to the farm after flowing beneath an unusual gated wooden bridge. That bridge carries the Centenary Way over the Stour and on to Shipston. The steep banks and overhanging branches of the trees make this ideal kingfisher habitat.

The name "Stour" is frequently given to rivers in lowland England. It is generally associated with slow flowing but forceful rivers, typical of the sort of rivers found in the rather flat midlands. Warwickshire's more famous river - the Avon - has a British rather than an English name. "Afon" means "river" in Welsh.

Walking north-east from Fell Mill Farm the wide prairie-like fields manage to swallow up any sign of footpaths, but close attention to

98

the map will bring you safely to the top of Idlicote Hill. Part of the way crosses a small ridge giving good views on either side. Another ridge - with trees adorning its top - may be lightly clad in the blue mists of a spring morning, whilst larks exult above and butterflies of every hue patrol the unkempt hedges.

In the copses and wooded corners of fields crows and wood pigeons busy themselves about their daily chores and tiny chiffchaffs announce their presence by insistently calling their name from deep within the undergrowth. A rather surprising feature of some of these woodlands is the fact that they are surrounded by deer fencing. If you are lucky you may spot the cause of this - a herd of deer quietly grazing in one of the fields. These deer are very prominent as some of them are almost white. They are very wary of people and as soon as they spot you they will move away. On the other hand, although you may be constantly surprised by the irregular pops and bangs of automatic bird scarers, neither the deer nor, ironically, the birds seem to take any notice of them at all.

A path passes close to the farm on Idlicote Hill with its red barns, and cherry trees buzzing with bees. Rather than nestling in the landscape the farm leaps out, its bright pink walls making it look somewhat like a giant liquorice allsort from a giant's bag of sweets. More in keeping with the locality is the distant spire of the church in Treddington, and the stone buildings of Whatcote with its small square church.

Climbing the first stile for some time and crossing the lane linking Honington with Whatcote brings you into the neatness of Idlicote. At the time of the Domesday book this place was home for 29 families (about 140 people) in 1911 the population was 101 and today it is just over 70. The hamlet is on top of a small rise opposite its eponymous hill. It has been described as "a little gem of the eighteenth century deep in the Warwickshire lanes." A large house plays neighbour to a truly delightful church almost hiding in an equally delightful churchyard.

Parts of the church date back to the 12th. century. Amongst its many features are a 14th. century three-decker pulpit - from which the minister and clerk conducted the congregation's worship - and an almost Byzantine 17th century carved oak font cover. The pulpit may be the only one of its type left in the country. The church is dedicated to St. James the Great and serves both Idlicote and Honington. There are many memorials to the Keighley-Peach family, a number of whom served the East India Company. These people may have influenced great events far away, but now they lie alongside the simpler folk who never had the opportunity to do so. It was the latter of whom Thomas Gray was thinking when he penned the lines (in his "Elegy in a Country Churchyard")

*"Perhaps in this neglected spot*

*is laid*
*Some heart once pregnant*
*with celestial fire;*
*Hands, that the rod of empire*
*might have sway'd,*
*Or waked to ecstasy the living*
*lyre."*

Externally the church has stone walls, in some places as much as three feet thick, and a tiny wooden shingled tower with a blue and gold clock which chimes the hours. Wild clematis scrambles over the shrubs in the churchyard and lesser celandine, pansies, primulas and speedwell spread their colour at your feet. At the right times of the year holly blue butterflies float around the holly and the ivy.

Near to the church is an octagonal, castellated tower and, most curiously, an abandoned outdoor swimming pool. How permission for the latter was ever obtained defies logic, and why it now lies so unlovely within such beautiful surroundings, only the local people will know. Close to it two plain brick columns support two carvings of baskets of fruit which in every sense of the words may be described as "over the top".

Leaving Idlicote to the north-west takes you past some majestic oaks, along a line of pollarded ash trees and through the remains of ridge and furrow fields. Missing hedgerows bring you back to the present as large open fields are traversed. Not only the hedgerows have gone - a clearly marked footpath on the Ordnance Survey map leading to the northern edge of Honington is impossible to locate. No matter, the lane leading back is pleasant enough to stroll along. Looking back up the hill the back of the large house is clearly visible, but the rest of Idlicote hides demurely amongst tall trees. More ridge and furrow provides the opportunity for squirrels to mimic speedboats as they bob into and out of sight in their sea of green grass.

So back to Honington with its chocolate-box thatched cottages, the sign proclaiming its successes in "Best Kept Village" competitions in the 1960's, and colourful gardens. The habit of many owners of these gardens to allow them, indeed encourage them, to spill into the village streets should not be encouraged as the presence of so many exotic species of plants detracts from the character of what should be a typical English scene.

Such small carping apart this area will repay the walker with its charm and peace, two qualities so often lacking in much of Britain today.

# The Brailes

MAP 151 REF. 316/393

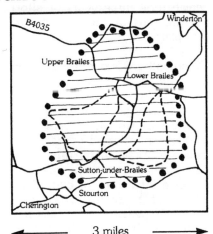

Parking possible by the church of St.George in Lower Brailes, on the B4035 four miles east of Chipston-On-Stour.

*This is beautiful walking country in the Warwickshire Cotswolds. Gentle hills enfold you in their shallow valleys - and in those valleys mixed farms provide a rich and varied landscape. Although cornfields dominate there are pastures grazed by sheep, horses and cattle, and other crops such as flax and beans. A walk in high summer is best, when the golden corn lies beneath blue skies and dark green hedgerows and trees trim the fields. Not all the paths are easy, and there are many stiles, electric fences and narrow planks laid over ditches.*

This part of the county is known as "the Feldon" - that is the field-land south of the River Avon. The fine church at Lower Brailes is called "the cathedral of the Feldon" and it is indeed a cut above the average village church. It is built in the Decorated style, and dates mainly from the middle of the 14th century. It was certainly not the first church on this site.

The first incumbent is listed as "Richard 1189". It is thought that Brailes had a Saxon church, and records of settlement here stretch back to pre Roman times. The surrounding churchyard is determinedly neat, and the main door beneath the tall tower is unfortunately painted in a somewhat out of character fashion with cream gloss paint. These things may have something to do with the "Best Kept Churchyard" certificates framed inside.

The church bristles with unusual features. Inside the porch there is a screen door designed to close across the half-open doorway, although the purpose of this is unclear. There is a working carillon which plays hymn tunes at appointed times. Around the west end of the church are a number of artefacts, including the early eighteenth century clock mechanism (now replaced with an electric movement) a basket-work wheelchair, a matchstick model of the church, and a tapestry panel which took three years of effort on the part of the villagers to complete.

A footpath leads out of the village into the fields around the lower slopes of Mine Hill. Old ridge and furrow soon gives way to modern ploughed fields. There are enough uncultivated corners and edges to allow many thistles to thrive. These in turn provide sustenance for a host of butterflies. There can be scores, if not hundreds, of peacock butterflies flitting from flower to flower on warm days in July and August. A dozen more species may join them, including painted lady, red admiral, large white, common blue and small skipper.

The footpaths are generally well signposted. They disappear in some of the corn fields, but often they may still be found cutting a narrow swathe through the ripening heads. Near to the top of the hill a couple of old barns take shelter in a small copse, and just past them wonderful views open out before you. This is what we like to think of as typical English countryside, but which is not now as typical as it used to be. Here there really is a patchwork of generally small fields, some green, some yellow or brown, all stitched together with lines of hedgerows, which are in turn pegged down with trees. Close at hand a yellowhammer makes its never ending plea for "a-little-bit-of-bread-and-no-cheeeeeese", nearby the pink flowers of water-loving great willowherb betray a spring line, and tractors and harvesters crawl across distant fields. The corn is not always as "clean" as the farmer would wish - wild oats, mayweed and poppies cling precariously to life before they too are harvested, and the edges of the paths are bright with the pretty pink and white flowers of field bindweed, the wild relative of morning glory.

A symptom of the age lies below along the banks of a small brook - Brailes Golf Course. No doubt built on land "set-aside" from agriculture its fertilised fairways gleam emerald like amongst the brown fields of harvest time. On the opposite hillside the Georgian style and name of New House Farm indicate that it was probably built during the time of the enclosures, when it could have been the first new building in the area for many years. (Brailes was once one of the three most important towns in the county, being much larger than it is today. There were two thousand householders in the parish in the reign of Edward V1 in the middle of the 16th century. It is known to have suffered great losses from the plague in 1603-1604.)

The path towards Sutton-under-Brailes turns into a green lane with rich hedgerows along its length. Hawthorn, blackthorn, brambles, elm and field maple scramble together, making it likely that this is an ancient hedgerow.

In one place our three most common thistles grow together by the side of the path: spear thistle with its sharply pointed leaves, globular flower heads and spiny stems; creeping thistle with its smaller flower heads and smooth stems; marsh thistle also with smaller flower heads but with prickly stems. The insects feeding on the flowers do not much care what sort of thistle they imbibe from, and butterflies may be abundant again here.

Sutton-under Brailes is a charming hamlet with stone cottages, one or two larger houses - such as Sutton Manor with its delightful wrought-iron gates - and a tall lime adorning the village green. Close to the green is a wonderful old tree stump. Of massive girth, and long dead, this grey and gnarled bole, studded with yellow lichens and twisted into grotesque shapes, now acts as a notice board for the village. A hundred rusty drawing pins pattern its bark about five feet from the ground.

The church shares its incumbent with St. George's in Lower Brailes, and its main door seems to have shared the same cream paint pot. It was not always so. This used to be an island of Gloucestershire, and the manor belonged to the monks of Westminster Abbey. This may account for the church being dedicated to the English martyr St.Thomas à Becket. The tower is set into the side of the church rather than being at the end, and the bell ropes hang down into the porch.

A path leaves the church through a small grazed orchard and climbs to a contour line about half way up Brailes Hill. On the way it passes a wet woodland full of whispering willows and poplars, as well as a motley collection of other planted trees, such as sycamore and various conifers. A pool has been created complete with a plastic heron. Whether this a decoy or a deterrent is uncertain. The path splits in two close to a small clump of trees consisting of some lonesome Scots pine being kept company by a couple of larches. One path goes off to Shipston, the other skirts around Brailes Hill above New House Farm.

The latter route takes you through swathes of cut-leaved geranium (with small pink flowers and bright red leaves) at the edge of a corn field, then between the modern barns of the farm and a sheep dip - which looks more like a sheep maze - and allows you a brief glimpse of the tall tower of St. George's before plunging down a steep-sided muddy gully. Tall trees arch overhead as you slip and slide towards Grove End. Wood avens, bluebells and foxgloves grow on the steep banks.

From the bottom of the gully it is possible to return via Upper Brailes or to do a circuit of the valley floor, taking in the new golf course. The path is difficult to find across New House Farm, but it is well signed across the golf course. Please take note of the warning notice about golf balls. The new club house is a rather uninteresting red brick, grey roofed building. It pays no regard to the local architecture, or to the use of local building materials. Apparently the planning authority thought that it should reflect the Georgian facade of New House Farm opposite, rather than the more Cotswold like buildings in the villages.

Lower Brailes is soon reached

again, the George Hotel waiting with its colourful tubs and window boxes. As you return to the car a glance up at the 110' high church tower will reveal four pennant like weathervanes, one on each of the four corners. If your route home should happen to take you through Chipping Campden you will see four almost identical weathervanes on its church.

# Whichford and Long Compton

## MAP 151 REF. 313/346

**Parking possible in the village of Whichford - there is no formal car park but the wide verge by the church is suitable. Whichford is buried in narrow lanes to the east of the A34 near to Long Compton, about four miles south east of Shipston-on-Stour.**

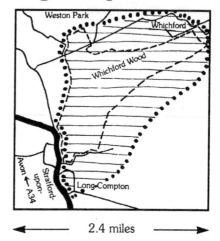

2.4 miles

*Fairly easy walking through the fields and woods of south Warwickshire. This is the edge of the Cotswolds with gentle climbs to rounded tops from where, it is said, you can see as many as 12 counties. The paths are well defined, but you will not find a signpost or a waymark to guide you. There are only one or two stiles or fences to climb. On some paths the mid-summer growth of vegetation will keep your legs wet long after the showers which anointed your head have cleared away.*

Whichford is a delightful village with stone cottages roofed with mossy tiles or low-eaved thatch. Roses and clematis scramble around doors and windows and up on to the rooves. The road past the church transforms itself into a track whilst leading you to Whichford Wood. An open gate beckons you into the cool shade beneath the trees, where the birdsong within contrasts with the gentle chimes of the church clock, or - at appropriate times - the more insistent pealing of its bells.

Whichford Wood is a wonderland of trees, flowers, birds and insects. As you pass through it centuries of woodland management unfold. Unlike many old woodlands this one is still actively managed. Each compartment can clearly be seen - one recently coppiced, another full of mature trees, another with rows of oaks in plastic Tulley tubes. It is unfortunate that those rows of new trees are geometrically arranged in straight lines. Even though they are broad-leaved trees and not conifers their regimentation detracts from the character of the wood. They are brooded over by tall standards of oak and ash and accompanied by field maple and hazel.

The woodland floor is a profusion of flowers in summer. In one part of the wood herb robert, bugle and pink campion tumble around the path, in another speedwell and vetches scramble for height, and in a third stitchwort and bluebells dominate. In early spring dog's mercury carpets the bare ground before the others have awoken from their winter slumbers.

Paths to Cherington and Stourton will be found over the 200 metre high Margett's Hill. Its flat top is intensively cultivated, leaving room for very few hedgerows, although there are some small copses. The far side of the hill affords extensive views over undulating countryside, with a tall church spire to the left and

Brailes Hill to the right. The skylarks, not being satisfied with the view from the hill top, rise higher still to see more of the county whilst sending cascades of sweet songs back to earth. The small woods in this area are well blessed with wych elm which in some places forms a low canopy over the paths.

Leaving Margett's Hill to the south-west reveals the wooded ridge above the village of Long Compton which nestles in a hollow below. The village is reached by traversing steeply sloping sheep pastures. The attentions of the sheep prevent all but the lowest growing plants thriving. One that does especially well is dove's-foot cranesbill, the flowers of which are tiny pink Geraniums shyly hiding in the grass.

Long Compton is full of attractive house and cottages, built mainly of local stone. Some have stone mullioned windows, some have thatched rooves and most have beautiful gardens. One may have an anachronistic name - it is called "Sumach Cottage" but was built in 1763. Would anyone in deepest Warwickshire have known about north American Sumachs in 1763, or has a later owner bestowed the name? A stream runs alongside the footpath of the A34 (strictly speaking now the A3400) with a good show of ivy-leaved toadflax clinging to the stonework of its channel.

The church - a fine looking building - is dedicated to St. Peter and

St. Paul. No information is offered about, it unlike most other village churches which provide either booklets, notices or information boards. This lack of enlightenment is particularly frustrating in this case as the church possesses a most unusual lych gate. This consists of a tiny odd shaped thatched cottage which incorporates the gate within itself. This must have a story to tell but what it is is left to conjecture.

A broad path takes you out of the village through a shallow valley to the south of Whichford Wood. Large fields with some enclosure hedgerows and sprinkled with small woods stretch out all around. It is rather like walking across the bottom of a giant saucer. The county boundary with Oxfordshire runs within about 200 yards of the path for some of its length. A short climb brings you back to Whichford Wood.

This side of the wood has some magnificent trees, including a huge beech (autographed by one "Steve Payne 1988") and a Turkey oak (recognised by the presence of hairs in all of its nodes, and in autumn by its "woolly" acorns). Another introduced species is sweet chestnut which has a coppice compartment to itself.

Rounding the end of the wood brings Whichford village into view, slumbering below in its blanket of trees whilst the larks sing a lullaby and Brailes Hill stands guardian-like behind. Any sign of the footpath now disappears, and to reach the village it is necessary to negotiate a fence or two and drop down through the meadows. There is plenty of young elm in the hedgerows here, and lady's smock, marsh thistle and meadow buttercup in the fields.

# Long Distance Footpaths

No book about walking would be complete without mention of the way-marked long distance routes which pass through the area concerned. In the West Midlands and Warwickshire there are three such routes. They are: the Beacon Way (which has the distinction of being Britain's shortest long distance footpath!) the Heart of England Way and the Centenary Way. Each of them will be encountered in the areas described in the book and brief information is given below.

## The Beacon Way:

This is a bold initiative by the Countryside Commission and Sandwell and Walsall Councils to give access to urban fringe countryside to the thousands of people living in the north east of the West Midlands. It is about 18 miles long and connects Chasewater in the north to the Sandwell Valley in the south. Car parking is available at many points along the route, particularly at Chasewater, Park Lime Pits, Barr Beacon and the Sandwell Valley. Plenty of buses pass close to access points throughout the length of the Way.

The route cleverly combines public footpaths, canal towpaths and areas of open countryside to thread its way from the heart of the conurbation to the edge of Cannock Chase. The southern portion from the Sandwell Valley to Park Lime Pits is fully waymarked, the northern portion remains to be done. This is not a serious impediment to walking the Way as much of the route north of Park Lime Pits lies along canal towpaths. A detailed leaflet is available from Walsall and Sandwell countryside ranger services.

The high point of the walk - literally and figuratively - is Barr Beacon, a small rise to the east of the conurbation but still within Walsall. Bearing in mind that the West Midlands is on the rim of the great plain of north-west Europe, it will not come as too much of a surprise to learn that the Beacon is the highest point between here and the Ural mountains. If you need convincing stand on the Beacon when an east wind is blowing in the winter.

## The Centenary Way:

Yes, it is a hundred miles long, and it is named to commemorate the 100th anniversary of Warwickshire County Council. The route was established by the Council in 1989 and connects many places in Warwickshire between its end points of Kingsbury Water Park and Meon Hill. All of Warwickshire's life, history and culture will be encountered along the Way.

The route encompasses public footpaths, bridleways, canal towpaths and disused railways. It has been divided into bite-sized chunks of about eight miles, each section having a leaflet describing the route and the features of

107

interest. These leaflets are available from country parks and information centres throughout Warwickshire. They give information on parking, public transport, pubs and cafes and, most usefully, circular walks linking to the main route. At both ends the Centenary Way connects with the Heart of England Way.

## The Heart of England Way:

Somewhat lugubriously subtitled "The West Midland's Regional Long Distance Footpath" this runs for 80 miles from Milford, on Cannock Chase, to Chipping Campden in Gloucestershire. It has been devised and promoted by the Heart of England Way Association, who publish a complete (almost step-by-step) guide. They acknowledge the recognition given by the three county councils of Staffordshire, Warwickshire and Gloucestershire, and the Metropolitan Borough Council of Solihull, and the assistance given by the Countryside Commission.

One of the principal features of the Way is its proximity to, but isolation from, the West Midlands Industrial conurbation. As the guide's author says: "The Way itself is not in the least urban but often in distant view or earshot are the sights and sounds of civilisation. I find this combination of the deeply rural with the urban fringe attractive and fascinating. I can reach the Way easily by bus or train for a day's walking, and just as easily get back from another place in the evening."

From Cannock Chase in the north the Way skirts around the eastern edge of Birmingham and the Black Country, passes through the Meriden Gap between Birmingham and Coventry, goes to Alcester, and then south across the Vale of Evesham to the northern Cotswolds. In doing so it connects two other long distance footpaths—the Staffordshire Way and the Cotswold Way.

# Places to Visit

It would be impossible to list all of the places of interest in the area covered by this book. There are scores of country houses and parks, mills, museums, working farms, historic sites, gardens and similar attractions in the two counties. A small selection is given below of some places which are either very close, or related, to one of the walking areas.

## Cotwall End Nature Centre
Catholic Lane
Sedgley
Dudley
West Midlands
15 acres of grass and woodland with a series of freshwater pools. Wild and domestic animals, craft shops.

## Black Country Museum*
Tipton Rd
Dudley
West Midlands
Reconstructed Victorian Black Country village, complete with authentic pub, bakery, chemist's shop, cobbled streets and period costumes. The buildings were all taken down on their original sites and rebuilt here.

## R.S.P.B. Nature Centre
Tanhouse Avenue
Hamstead
Sandwell
West Midlands
One of the RSPB's most popular reserves with both people and birds - it is in the top 20 reserves in the country for both variety of birds and numbers of human visitors. Hides overlooking open water and marshland.

## Park Farm*
Lodge Rd
Sandwell Valley
West Bromwich
West Midlands
A restored early 17th century farm built with an enclosed courtyard. The farming practices of the 19th century are demonstrated using authentic breeds of stock. Many other attractions, including a kitchen garden and a detailed display about the priory which used to be nearby.

## Weoley Castle*
Alwold Rd
Birmingham
West Midlands
Ruins of a moated manor house, the earliest remains dating from the twelfth century. Small museum relating to the site. Restricted opening hours.

## Sarehole Mill
Cole Bank Rd
Birmingham
West Midlands
A restored and working mill on the River Cole. The miller here at the turn of the century was the inspiration for one of J.R. Tolkien's characters. Open in the afternoons from March to November.

**Church Leyes Farm***
Napton-on-the-Hill
Warwickshire
Non-commercial organic working
farm.
Open every day except Saturday.

**Moorwood Rare Breed
Leisure Farm***
Oldbury Rd
Hartshill
Nr Nuneaton
Warwickshire
30 rare and traditional breeds of
farm animals living and working
on the farm. Play area, gift shop,
spinning demonstrations.

* Charge for entry.

**Shire Horse Centre and Farm
Park***
Clifford Rd
Stratford-Upon-Avon
Warwickshire
20 shire horses together with
other farm animals and an aviary.
Picnic area, nature trail, riverside
walk.

**Edgehill Battle Museum***
The Estate Yard
Farnborough Hall
Farnborough
Banbury
Oxfordshire
Displays of arms, armour and cos-
tumes of the late 17th century, to-
gether with models, dioramas and
maps of the battle.

# Tourist Information Centres

The value of TICs to the visitor cannot be over-emphasised. They are unrivalled mines of local information and if their staff are unable to supply the necessary information their local knowledge will invariably provide an alternative source. Do not make the mistake of assuming they are "mere" bed-booking agencies alone.

**Birmingham**
Convention & Visitor Bureau, 2 City Arcade, B2 4TX.
Tel: 021 643 2514.

Convention & Visitor Bureau, National Exhibition Centre, B40 1NT.
Tel: 021 780 4312.

Birmingham International Airport Information Desk, B26 3QJ.
Tel: 021 767 7145/7146.

**Brierly Hill**
Management Suite, Merry Hill Centre, Pedmore Road, West Midlands Y5 1SY. Tel: 0384 481141.

**Coventry**
Bayley Lane, West Midlands CV1 5RN. Tel: 0203 832303/832304.

**Dudley**
39 Churchill Precinct, West Midlands  DY2 7BL. Tel: 0384 250333.

**Kenilworth**
The Library, 11 Smalley Place, Warwickshire  CV8 1OG.
Tel: 0926 52595/50708.

**Rugby**
The Library, St. Mathews Street, Warwickshire  CV21 3BZ.
Tel: 0788 535348.

**Solihull**
Central Library, Homer Road, West Midlands  B91 3RG.
Tel: 021 704 6130/6134.

**Stratford-upon-Avon**
Bridgefoot, Warwickshire  CV37 6GW. Tel: 0789 293127.

**Stourbridge**
The Library, Crown Centre. Tel: 0384 394004.

**Wolverhampton**
18 Queen Square, West Midlands  WV1 1TO. Tel: 0902 312051.

# Other Useful Organisations

The West Midlands and Warwickshire have two wildlife trusts who are members of the Royal Society for Nature Conservation's Wildlife Trusts' Partnership. They are:

**The Urban Wildlife Trust**
(Working in Birmingham and the Black Country)
Unit 213
Jubilee Trades Centre
130 Pershore St
Birmingham B5 6ND
Telephone: 021 666 7474


**WARNACT** (the Warwickshire Nature Conservation Trust)
Brandon Marsh Nature Centre
Brandon Lane
Coventry CV3 3GW
Telephone: 0203 302912


Details of other organisations, local authority countryside management services and general information available from:


**WMEN** (West Midlands Environment Network)
23 Hamstead Rd.
Birmingham B19 1BX
Telephone: 021 515 2300

# Recommended Reading

**Bread Upon the Waters.** (An account of canal life).
David Blagrove. J.M.Pearson and Son.

**Food for Free.** Richard Mabey. Collins.

**The Heart of England Way.**
John Roberts. The Heart of England Way Association.

**The Making of the British Countryside.**
Ron Freethy. David & Charles.

**The Roadside Wildlife Book.**
Richard Mabey. David and Charles.

**Wildlife Walkabouts: Birmingham and the Black Country.**
Peter Shirley. Wayside Books.

**The Wild Side of Town.**
Chris Baines. BBC Publications / Elm Tree Books.

**Woodland Walks in Central England.**
Gerald Wilkinson. Webb and Bower / Ordnance Survey.

**Wren's Nest National Nature Reserve Geological Handbook & Field Guide.**
English Nature / Dudley Council.

# Ramblers Association

The Ramblers' Association exists to pursue four main aims: to promote rambling, to protect footpaths, to seek public access to open country and to defend the natural beauty of the countryside. Set up in 1935, the association has a large membership and more than 330 local RA groups. Members receive copies of the association's quarterly colour magazine and our annual Rambler's Yearbook and Accommodation Guide. In addition, they may borrow OS maps from our extensive library and are eligible for discounts in certain outdoor equipment stores.

Local groups organise regular programmes of walks as well as practical footpath work and social evenings. To campaign with even greater success, we need to increase our membership so that we are seen to be truly representative of all those who love rambling in the countryside.

For more information, please contact:
The Ramblers' Association,
1–5 Wandsworth Road,
London SW8 2XX.
Telephone: 071 582 6878.

**The Ramblers**

# Open Spaces Society

The Open Spaces Society, formally the Commons, Open Spaces and Footpaths Preservation Society, was founded in 1865 and is Britain's oldest national conservation body. We campaign to protect common land, village greens, open spaces and public paths and your right to enjoy them. We advise local authorities and the public on common land and public path law, and give support to campaigns on a local level.

Members have instant access to the society's advisory service; receive the society's informative journal three times a year and are entitled to discount on the society's publications. For more information please contact:
The Open Spaces Society,
25a Bell Street,
Henley on Thames,
Oxon RG9 2BA.
Telephone: (0491) 573535.
(Registered charity no. 214753).

**THE
OPEN SPACES
SOCIETY**

# About the Author

Peter Shirley is Director of the Urban Wildlife Trust - the Royal Society for Nature Conservation's Wildlife Trusts' Partnership trust for Birmingham and the Black Country. He has had a life long interest in wildlife and the countryside. His work for the Trust involves him in issues related to nature conservation, countryside management, public access, interpretation and legislation. He has been writing and broadcasting about these subjects for more than ten years.

Peter's special interest is the study of insects, particularly insect / plant relationships. He has been Chair of the British Association of Nature Conservationists, and is a member of the British Plant Gall Society, the Amateur Entomologists' Society, the RSPB and Sandwell Valley Field Naturalists' Club.

Peter lives in West Bromwich with his wife Dot and their two sons Christopher and Julien.

# Notes

# Notes

# Notes